MW01121780

REALITY AND BEYOND THIS WORLD

A BEGINNER'S GUIDE TO SELF ACTUALISATION

FIONA FAILLA

Disclaimer

The content provided in this book is for information purposes only. It is not intended to
serve as medical advice or to diagnose, treat, cure, or prevent any physical or mental
health conditions. The practices, ideas, and suggestions within this book are based on
the author's personal experiences and research. They are not a substitute for
professional medical advice, diagnosis, or treatment. If you have any concerns about
your mental, physical, or emotional health, please consult a qualified healthcare
provider or medical practitioner before attempting any techniques or following any
suggestions outlined in this book.

Neither the author nor the publisher shall be liable for any adverse effects, injuries, or
damages resulting from the application of the information provided herein. Always
seek the advice of your physician or other qualified healthcare provider with any
questions you may have regarding a medical condition.

To those whom the universe has aligned on this shared path. May we ask questions, seek answers, and support each other on this journey together.

CONTENTS

When I was in business, I had the motto,
'We are a helping hand on your business journey'.

Now I have the motto,

'I am there to be a helping hand on your life journey'.

INTRODUCTION - A NEW BEGINNING

Growing up in Melbourne, Australia, during the 1970s, as the oldest child of Catholic Italian immigrants in a suburb with few other immigrants was challenging. I had to balance the constantly changing Australian way of life with my Italian upbringing. Since our extended family was all interstate and overseas, we spent important holidays like Easter and Christmas with friends and the community my parents were part of.

My first language was Italian, and I spent a few years in childcare run by Italian Catholic sisters. I would arrive before 7 a.m. and attend church with the sisters daily. I didn't learn English until I started primary school, which was a big shock because I only spoke Italian until then. Most of the students at my primary school were Australian, and I didn't fit in. I struggled to learn English since I only spoke it at school, and everyone around me at home spoke Italian. I worked hard to learn English and eventually stopped speaking Italian until I was a teenager. In high school, after visiting our extended family overseas and realising I had forgotten the language, I decided to relearn Italian. I learned at a young age that I had to assimilate to fit in.

It wasn't easy being constantly teased by the boys down the street, who called me a 'wog' and other names, telling me I didn't belong in Australia even though I was born here. Every time I walked or rode my bike to my friend's house, I dreaded passing the house where the bullies lived. I would quickly race past and feel relieved if they weren't there. This continued for years. I remember my mother always telling me not to worry and trying to comfort me when I cried from their taunts.

Like many others, my parents worked hard to build a comfortable life in Australia. Initially, they worked two jobs before starting their own business in ladies' wear manufacturing, where I helped as much as possible.

When I was thirteen, I calculated and paid the staff and organised bill payments. They eventually closed the business when ladies' wear production moved overseas, and brands no longer wanted to pay Australian rates to manufacturers.

I attended an all-girls Catholic college, where my small group of friends shared the same cultural background. Although I was friendly with everyone, I was very shy. My close friends understood our culture, and our parents held the same ideals. As a teenager, I struggled to talk to boys because they seemed like a foreign species to me. I even bought a book called *How to Talk to Boys*. The funny thing is, a few years later, I met my husband, and we have been together ever since.

I was lucky to have a happy childhood with my parents despite having no other family nearby. Some of my friends were not so lucky and suffered emotional and physical abuse. It was overwhelming for them to endure this as children while pretending to the community that everything was fine. Seeing and hearing about their struggles made me realise that our childhood experiences shape us as we grow up. It's important to address and heal from these negative patterns to ensure a healthier and more positive future for everyone.

At eighteen, having grown up in the clothing industry, I decided to open a ladies' wear store. A few years later, I started a fabric and wool shop in the same shopping centre. With a strong work ethic instilled by my parents, I managed these businesses for a time. I closed the ladies' wear store the day before my wedding and negotiated the sale of the fabric and wool shop while I was in the hospital giving birth to my eldest daughter.

When my eldest child started kindergarten in 1999, I volunteered to become treasurer of the kindergarten. I implemented many changes due to the introduction of the new tax system, GST (Goods and Services Tax) which was rolled out the following year. I taught myself how to use accounting software and understand GST rules, which required many hours of work. This eventually allowed me to start a bookkeeping business, where I juggled work, home life and further education.

In 2003, I established my business just before my twins began primary school. I gradually built it up, eventually hiring staff and moving to an office. I became a successful BAS Agent, bookkeeper and accounting software trainer. I thoroughly enjoyed supporting business owners, offering them advice, and training them. Many of my clients stuck with me for years, and I cherished every moment I got to help them with their businesses.

During those years, my husband decided to open a tyre and mechanical shop. I mainly assisted him with back-office tasks. Sometimes, I'd pitch in at the front of the store, where I quickly gained a solid understanding of tyres and expertise in the field.

In March 2020, Melbourne, Australia, experienced a series of government-enforced lockdowns that lasted a total of 267 days, making it one of the toughest lockdowns worldwide. During that time, I had clients calling me in tears as their businesses suffered. As time went on, they lost hope as it seemed we might never reopen.

Meanwhile, the government provided lifelines for business owners, which I quickly learned about and helped clients apply for if they were eligible. My adult children, who were all at home during this time, could recite by heart the information I repeated from morning to night as I sat at my desk in the living room. Much of this work was done without charging a fee because I deeply empathised with my clients who were struggling financially and relied on my support. Businesses were closing down at record-breaking times around Victoria, which was devastating. This experience shifted my perspective on life, but over time, it left me emotionally drained.

During this period, I began questioning our reality and wondering if there was more to life than what we experienced physically. I started to discover that there was indeed more. Then, in September 2021, my mother passed away after battling illnesses for years. It was a challenging time because she passed away during lockdown, making it difficult for my father to receive government support. Fortunately, my father lived nearby, so I was able to be there for him and offer support.

I became so exhausted that I caught COVID. I became seriously ill, and everything I once knew seemed to vanish from my mind. I remember days where I would just lie there staring at the ceiling, struggling to focus or even put two sentences together. It took me months to get back on track, but with the support of healthcare and alternative practitioners, my health slowly started to improve.

Even though I still felt off, I returned to work and tried to catch up, but it seemed like the challenges just kept piling up. These challenges, along with all the deeply personal events, triggered a line of thinking: *'What is really important, and what really matters in life?'*

Working long hours, seven days a week, was not sustainable. The joy was draining from my life, and I knew I needed a change. It was a difficult decision—a decision to leave a highly successful, award-winning business, firmly attached to financial and reputational success after so much hard work, and step into the complete unknown. Gulp. But herein lies the key—I followed my intuition, and the instruction was clear: space was required for clarity to emerge. That's when my life took a huge turn, and I sold my business in September 2022.

It took about a year before I found clarity on the next steps. During that year, I embarked on a profound journey of self-discovery. I pored over countless books and research, becoming an avid seeker of truth and exploring what lay beyond the everyday. I delved into various forms of alternative healing and engaged with practitioners who provided invaluable guidance and support. Each experience deepened my understanding of myself and my spiritual path.

I had been seeing alternative practitioners who were very helpful to me, and I couldn't have gone on this journey without them. Then, during a hypnosis session, something new and exciting revealed itself. By December 2023, clarity emerged quickly! I felt a strong message from my higher self: I must write a book to help others with the knowledge I had been gifted. Once published, this would lead to selling my husband's business.

Write a book? I was a bookkeeper, not a book writer! The task felt overwhelming, and I doubted myself. But the urging wouldn't stop; it was relentless. Was I letting my ego get in the way? If I chose to believe my ego's self-doubt chatter, I was blocking the path. So, I forged on.

This was a significant task, starting a new chapter in my life that was both inspiring and daunting.

Not everyone around me agreed with or supported my choice to write this book. Some questioned whether I was truly certain about it. But I knew this was the right course. It required courage, determination and a deep understanding of my purpose to hold my ground.

And here you are, just as I was, taking the first step toward a happier and more fulfilling life by reading this book!

This book is designed to help those seeking joy and fulfilment. It offers shared knowledge and guidance to inspire you. Inside, you'll find techniques to help you explore new paths and embrace the true essence of who you are and who you want to become.

In a world where people are sensing a shift and growing curious, the message was clear: there was a need for a book that touched on these spiritual topics without overwhelming readers or presenting polarising concepts. I am no spiritual guru, but I aim to provide a guide that offers simple practices, along with some fascinating scientific research. This book seeks to unlock our wisdom about life and how to live authentically, helping us discover the best version of ourselves and the life we desire.

When we begin recognising the signs around us and exercising discernment in our life choices, we can start a new way of living. We can understand that we have free will and can live our lives in ways that can either benefit or harm us. There is beauty in truly knowing that we will all reach our intended destination in our own time.

You can read the chapters in the order they appear or choose the ones that resonate with you. Keep an open mind and try the practices that suit your current needs. Feel free to revisit the book multiple times; different parts may stand out to you at different stages of life. What's relevant now may change over time.

I hope this book helps you make the necessary changes to align with your desired path and achieve your lifetime aspirations.

Fiona

PART I
FOUNDATIONS OF SELF-ACTUALISATION

Welcome to Part One: Foundations of Self-Actualisation. Here, we establish the groundwork for comprehending and embracing the concept of self-actualisation.

We'll discuss the signs that help you recognise the beginning of a spiritual journey, explore how to examine your past and future selves and suggest practical steps for this transformation. We can live more meaningful lives by aligning our actions with our core values and goals. We will examine techniques to uncover your authentic identity—your fundamental self—and find ways to help you identify your current situation. Then, we will guide you in reconnecting with your true self. There is also some scientific insight providing a factual basis for many topics.

Each chapter builds on the last, offering insights and resources to help you get closer to reaching your full potential. Part Two empowers you with tools to engage with these theories and helps you discover your life's purpose on the path to self-actualisation. Part Three is intended to challenge your perspective and encourage you to question the world we live in.

Remember, self-actualisation is a journey, not a destination. It's about the experiences and growth along the way.

SELF-ACTUALISE

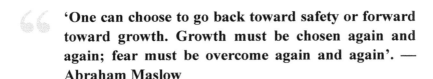'One can choose to go back toward safety or forward toward growth. Growth must be chosen again and again; fear must be overcome again and again'. — Abraham Maslow

Our Earth is experiencing significant changes, leading to unrest worldwide. This is the time for us all to consciously awaken our minds and raise our vibration. As humans, we, too, will change, adjusting our conscious state of being.

The transition is not necessarily physical but can impact our physical body as we shift our mindset and way of being. For some, this change can happen faster than for others depending on how open we are to do the work.

You may hear terms like 'dimensions' and 'multiverse'. These terms often appear in Hollywood movies and spiritual discussions. You might wonder what they mean and how they relate to our evolving view of the world. Our reality encompasses everything within our visual, tactile and measurable scope. Scientists study tangible physical reality similarly.

In contrast, our spiritual reality includes things we can't measure, such as thoughts, feelings and the soul. This aspect of reality is grounded in personal experiences and perceptions, making it challenging for scientists to study it in the same way as they do the physical world. These realities intertwine, and when we embark on a spiritual path, we begin to see how the two intersect. It isn't always easy to be open-minded to a reality we can't see, hear, touch or smell!

When we explore reality, we must understand our basic needs. Abraham Maslow, a very influential American psychologist, is well known for creating Maslow's Hierarchy of Needs. Maslow's theory explains these needs and helps us see how they relate to both our physical and spiritual lives.

This theory explains that we all have basic needs which must be met before we can focus on reaching our full potential. Maslow illustrated these needs in the shape of a pyramid. At the base of the pyramid are our fundamental needs for survival, such as food and safety. As we move up the pyramid, the needs shift toward personal fulfilment, including the need for love and respect from others. Ultimately, the highest level is reaching our full potential, which Maslow called self-actualisation.

Many fields of expertise have accepted his ideas. They are not solely based on psychology. They also help us understand what drives human behaviour.

As we understand the different dimensions, including the spiritual ones, we see how they connect to Maslow's Hierarchy. Moving up this hierarchy, individuals reach a point where they comprehend and transcend their basic needs. Let's investigate further:

1. **Physiological needs**: These are the fundamental necessities for human survival, such as air, water, food and shelter.
2. **Safety needs**: Once physiological needs are met, the focus shifts to seeking safety, security and stability.

3. **Belongingness**: Following safety, individuals seek a sense of belonging and acceptance within relationships and social groups.
4. **Esteem**: At this level, the need for self-esteem and respect becomes predominant. This includes feelings of accomplishment and recognition from others.

Maslow's Hierarchy of Needs

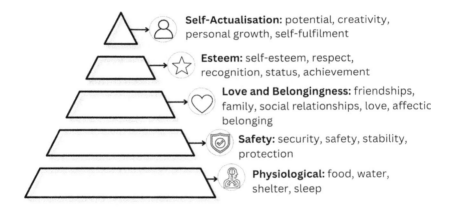

Self-Actualisation: potential, creativity, personal growth, self-fulfilment

Esteem: self-esteem, respect, recognition, status, achievement

Love and Belongingness: friendships, family, social relationships, love, affectic belonging

Safety: security, safety, stability, protection

Physiological: food, water, shelter, sleep

At the top of Maslow's pyramid is self-actualisation, where individuals strive to realise their fullest potential. Beyond this stage, Maslow identified the realm of self-transcendence, a state where individuals live authentically, manifest their values and bring their envisioned future into the present. This leads to a profound connection with themselves and the world around them.

Green et al. (2007) and many other scholars suggest a solid framework of strategies to help people achieve self-actualisation. They propose that some of the following may aid in reaching self-actualisation and beyond. They are:

- **Art** – Utilising art as a creative outlet helps people express their emotions
- **Thinking outside the box** – Embracing the idea that there is no clear-cut either/or, but understanding how to work with and manage polarities
- **Structures** – Providing structures that stimulate individuality, autonomy and initiative within a culture; striking a balance leads to better satisfaction and motivation

Maslow reinforced this view by observing that individuals who attain advanced levels of personal development—what he referred to as the 'farther reaches of human nature'—tend to have a keen perception of reality and truth. They are more open to the nuances of reality and truth and are clear about what is right and wrong. They make ethical decisions more quickly and confidently (Maslow, 1971).

INDICATORS THAT WE ARE ON OUR AWAKENING JOURNEY

On our awakening journey, we will encounter many obstacles. Each one we overcome brings us a step closer to our goal, which is finding love, unity, compassion and freedom from judgement.

Questioning and reevaluating our beliefs is no easy feat! I touch on this extensively in this book, as nearly every instance involves certain beliefs and ideals that must be understood and reassessed to alter our perceptions and let go, allowing us to truly experience life through a lens of love and gratitude.

Some of us need to change the beliefs we learned as children. We may now be unsure of who we are. It can be a very confusing time as we may need to reevaluate our lives and what we want from them.

I like to imagine the beliefs and ideologies we absorb are like a house built from the experiences and influences we've encountered throughout our lives. From the moment we are born, our surroundings —including nurture or lack thereof, family culture, education, and society—begin to lay the foundation. Each interaction, piece of advice and observed behaviour adds another brick, shaping the rooms of our house.

As we grow, this house becomes more elaborate. Early childhood provides the basic structure: the walls are formed by what we experience. Our interactions with caregivers and the world serve as the first coat of paint, colouring our perception of the world. Education and friendships during our formative years add new rooms and decorations, each representing new ideas and perspectives. These beliefs may manifest as shame, guilt or fear, or they may represent a view that isn't aligned with our future self or who we truly are. Why? Because shame, guilt and fear are heavy in energy and hold us back.

By the time we reach adulthood, our house is a complex structure, with each room reflecting a different aspect of our identity and beliefs. Some rooms might be cosy and inviting, filled with beliefs that empower us and make us feel safe. Others might be cluttered or even neglected, representing outdated or harmful ideologies that no longer serve us well.

Letting go of old beliefs is much like renovating our house. We might need to knock down some walls, clear out the clutter and redesign the space to better reflect who we are today. It's all about examining each room—each belief—and deciding whether it still fits the life we want. Just as a house needs regular upkeep, our belief system benefits from checking in and making changes.

By recognising that our environment shapes our beliefs, we can take charge and make conscious changes. We can remodel our inner space to create an atmosphere that truly supports our growth and well-being.

Letting go of experiences and old patterns that play out in our lives is a choice. We must acknowledge the pattern, honour the experience, and release it. Reacting in the same old way to situations means we have yet to learn the lesson needed to move forward. We must challenge these feelings to pave the beautiful pathway to freedom.

This can feel like starting over. It is, in a sense, but remember, this brave choice has led you here. You are reading these words exactly when you are supposed to. You have already started your journey.

Feeling overwhelmed by who we are and what we want in life is part of the process. Abraham Maslow said that self-actualisation is becoming 'all you can become'. Much of this has to do with our egoic self—the way we identify with ourselves. In the chapter 'Leave Your Ego at the Door', we examine our ego. When we start to gently strip it away, we are left with our raw, authentic selves, which can be harrowing for some.

This is also known as the *Dark Night of the Soul*. Eckhart Tolle describes it as 'a term used to describe what one could call a collapse of a perceived meaning in life... an eruption into your life of a deep sense of meaninglessness'. Sometimes, we may do research that answers our questions. However, this can also leave us feeling overwhelmed.

Are You Feeling Confused by Everything You See and Hear: What Is Real?

Overcoming fear can be an arduous journey. The first step to alleviating it is to use the process of identification and elimination. One huge source of fear in our modern world is the news. If the constant stream of gloomy news causes despair, then take a detox. Identify the sources in your life that bring in negativity. This doesn't mean you shouldn't stay informed. Instead, you should be deliberate and find alternative channels to receive your news that inform but don't overwhelm.

When we encounter negative or fear-based news, we must ask ourselves: *What is there to learn from this? What benefit does it serve?*

Is there anything I can do about this situation? Throughout human history, we have never been more bombarded with such a vast amount of international information, including acts of atrocities that we often feel powerless to resolve or address. It may sound like ignorance, but I implore you: what you watch, you absorb, and what you absorb, your body feels and stores. Is there a better way to use your energy or to be of service? Or is there a cause locally you can support? We can't always have blinders on, but we must be mindful of what we consume.

When we feel fear, we must pause and ask ourselves: *Where is this fear coming from? What is triggering it? Is it a fear of the future?* Perhaps it presents no obvious source. *Is it from a past life? Could it be driven by our subconscious?*

Reflect on this: If the future is not yet made, then why waste our precious energy worrying about something that hasn't happened yet? We live in a heavily divided world, and it is easy to lean into the fear driven by all sides; it is important to enjoy being part of the whole, part of humanity.

Physical Changes

Physical changes can occur during the process of awakening. These might include body aches, sore joints, headaches, blurry vision, hot flashes, skin changes and weight loss or gain, amongst others. These symptoms may not all happen simultaneously. For me, blurry vision was a catalyst for some reflection. I had 20/20 vision all my life, but my eyesight deteriorated. I always had headaches and migraines, but they continued despite my best efforts to stop them. The book elaborates on this connection further in the chapter on 'Emotions and Ailments'.

When we are sick, we should determine whether the symptoms are related to awakening or caused by something else. If symptoms persist, always seek medical attention from a licensed practitioner.

Are You Fatigued?

Fatigue is one of the obvious and significant symptoms during awakening. Sometimes, our internal energy systems initiate change before our conscious mind has caught up. Both our bodies and minds work very hard to make these changes. Why? Using the earlier analogy, those house renovations require a LOT of extra energy. If we were already tired before, then this fatigue can be exacerbated. I suffered a lot of fatigue. Seeing my acupuncturist and taking Chinese herbs from my therapist worked well for me. Accepting the need to stop and rest was a crucial step. It may sound obvious, but often, we ignore tiredness and push through. Sometimes, I would experience the opposite effect and have an influx of energy. On those days, I would accomplish as much as possible while also keeping some in reserve.

Do You Feel Drawn to Nature?

I've always felt a strong pull toward nature. I love relaxing at the beach, walking in the park or listening to a waterfall. These places bring me so much peace and calm. See the chapters 'Water H_2O' and 'Nature' for more of our Earth's wonders and how to tune in—wanting to be outdoors more often. You might feel the need to escape to these peaceful spots in search of some tranquillity. This connection to nature is a big sign of spiritual awakening, indicating you're syncing with the Earth's natural rhythms. If you feel the urge to be outside, go for it! Being in nature can nurture your soul and help you feel grounded, bringing a sense of peace and clarity to your journey. You can also immerse yourself in natural environments by using some of the tools from Part Two of this book. Nature is a powerful amplifier and healer.

Do You Experience Déjà Vu?

Most of us have felt déjà vu—that uncanny feeling that we've been in the same place doing the same thing before. We often laugh it off or stand in awe, but you may not have connected it to an awakening journey. Déjà vu can certainly be a sign that you are undergoing a spiritual transformation. While it can be overwhelming at first, take a moment when it happens to pause and reflect on the present moment and what you might be thinking about. You may even want to take notes. In 'Remembering Who We Are', we discuss this *'I've been here before'* sensation in more detail.

Are You Experiencing Shifts in Your Relationships?

As our energy shifts and we become more aware, our relationships can and do change. For instance, out of nowhere, you might find it hard to relate to a lifelong best friend. Perhaps their focus is on going out and having fun, which no longer holds interest for you. This shift can be confusing for the person experiencing it. We may also force ourselves to stay the same, but this is not a wise move as you will discover in the subsequent chapters.

There is no question that a shift in your alignment can provoke some negative responses. People sense energy shifts on many levels, and change can be a struggle. It is natural for those who have known and loved us for a long time to be startled by changes in our energy and attitude. Remember, this is a reflection of their internal responses and possibly their emotional journey, triggers and experiences, from which they, too, must learn from.

So, what can you do in a situation when others project their discomfort on you? Compassion, first and always. Remember that they are on a journey, too, and as you have shifted vibrationally, it may take time for others to get used to the new you. A practical step is to envision yourself surrounded by white light, particularly if you are feeling overwhelmed by someone's negativity. You can also ask your angels for protection. We all have guardian angels who always help us when we ask or need them, so be sure to call on them. There are also powerful archangels that can assist you. Some of the major archangels are Michael, whom you can call upon for protection, Gabriel, if you are having trouble communicating and Raphael for healing and guidance.

You may find yourself wanting to have more profound conversations with friends and family. See if they are curious about or on board with your new way of thinking. The people we surround ourselves with may change, reflecting our positive energy and shared interests.

Are You Trusting Your Intuition?

Trusting ourselves, particularly our intuition, can be difficult. Often, intuition manifests as a gut feeling. If something doesn't feel right, our intuition is usually guiding us. Intuition may come as a subtle niggle or a faint whisper that something is amiss. However, over time, the noise and pace of modern life can drown out these quiet nudges, making it hard to listen to our instincts. Ignoring our intuition can lead to regret, as we often realise in hindsight that we should have trusted our gut. Intuition is a deeply embedded mechanism developed through evolution. Despite its ancient origins, many of us have lost touch with how to trust or heed its signals.

The inspiring healer and author Louise Hay has a famous quote that is quite apt here: *'I trust the intelligence within me. Whatever is happening out there is only a mirror of my own limited thinking. I now choose to let my heart guide me. I am safe'.*

Are You Experiencing Vivid or Lucid Dreams?

Vivid or lucid dreaming can also be a sign of your awakening journey. The chapter entitled 'Dreams' explores these experiences in greater detail and highlights how the veil between our world and the world beyond is thinning. Your dreams may become more frequent and intense and are worth paying attention to!

Beginning a spiritual awakening and the process of self-actualisation is a deeply personal and transformative experience. It involves navigating changes in beliefs, emotions and physical sensations. By recognising and understanding these signs, we can better prepare ourselves for the challenges and growth that lie ahead. So trust your intuition. Embrace your true self. Seek unity and compassion. These steps will help you to move closer to your full potential.

REMEMBERING WHO WE ARE

 'We are not human beings having a spiritual experience; we are spiritual beings having a human experience'. — Pierre Teilhard de Chardin

We are souls who have come into this world to immerse ourselves in the vast adventure of human existence. Our souls chose this journey to experience the full spectrum of reality. We are here to feel human touch, to dance, to love, to run and to taste our favourite foods. But as we know from our travels thus far, it's not just about the joy. Life is indeed a spectrum, a grand story that, like every good story, includes shade as well as light. We live in a world of contrasts. There is laughter and tears, triumphs and heartbreaks. Each moment teaches us valuable lessons. To feel anything is to engage in a great adventure. It is to be human. Put simply, we are here to learn.

I love this quote from Ram Dass: '*We learn how to love the universe just the way it is... we are all one consciousness in many bodies, we are one family*'.

The world can feel heavy, and it's easy to get caught up in its ordinary nature—the daily comings and goings, tasks, responsibilities and the mundane. We become disconnected from our origins, forgetting that we are powerful beings with infinite potential, here with purpose. When we awaken, we begin to question and realise that we are more than this body. We begin to feel a beautiful inkling (and sometimes a fearful one) that there is more to this!

Part of our spiritual journey is remembering who we are.

Remembering who we are helps us make better decisions, leading us to a more fulfilled and authentic life.

We are connected to the power of the universe, an energy of infinite potential and possibilities. There is a symbiotic relationship between our earthly experience and the universe. When our mind, body and heart are in tune with the frequency and vibrations of the universe, we exist in harmony as one. Discovering your true self and forging genuine connections allows you to align with your inner path.

PAST LIVES

Have you ever felt a strange connection to a place or person? Or experienced déjà vu so strong that it seemed like more than a coincidence? These moments might hint that we have lived multiple lives. Reincarnation is the belief that after death, our soul begins a new life in a different body. This idea is central to many spiritual traditions worldwide, suggesting that our experiences are part of an endless cycle of birth, life, death and rebirth. Our actions and growth in past lives shape this cycle.

Embracing the idea of reincarnation allows us to view life as a continuous journey of learning and evolution. It offers a profound connection to the mysteries of existence and spiritual development. Why do we reincarnate? Life on Earth is complex, and self-actualisation transforms its highs and lows into gifts. Trauma or unresolved issues from past lives may affect our current behaviours and emotions. By exploring our past lives, we can uncover the answers we seek and find healing.

Exploring past lives can bring emotional and physical healing as old, unresolved issues come to light. It enhances self-awareness, revealing patterns and habits that affect our current lives. This process can ease fears and anxieties, making us feel as though a significant burden has been lifted while also fostering spiritual growth. It helps us find our life's purpose and deepens our connection with the universe. In the end, this journey empowers us, boosting confidence, self-esteem and a sense of purpose in our destiny.

REVIEWING OUR PAST LIVES CAN GIVE US THE FOLLOWING BENEFITS:

- **Healing**: This can be both emotional and physical, as unresolved issues may come forward.
- **Self-awareness**: A deeper understanding of any patterns, habits or issues may come to the surface.
- **Relief:** Releasing fears and anxiety tied to past-life experiences can feel like lifting a heavy weight.
- **Spiritual growth**: This process can help us discover our life's purpose and deepen our connection with the universe.
- **Empowerment:** Understanding our destiny and enhancing our confidence and self-esteem can lead to a sense of empowerment.

There are several ways to explore our past lives. Dreams can serve as portals to our past experiences, offering glimpses into previous existences. Meditation, too, can help access these memories. You can learn more about these techniques in their respective chapters.

HYPNOSIS

Past-life regression therapy, or hypnosis, involves a trained therapist who guides you into a relaxed state to access past-life memories. This guided form of treatment helps you understand and integrate these experiences. It's important to find a reputable practitioner before undertaking this therapy.

HIGHER SELF

Have you ever wondered who's behind your thoughts? This question suggests the existence of an observer—a conscious presence—beyond our thoughts. This observer doesn't create the thoughts; it simply witnesses them. This is your higher self or soul.

Think of your higher self as a backseat driver on your life's journey. It's always there, offering gentle nudges and wisdom, even if we don't always notice. It might feel like we're ignoring a soft whisper from the backseat. Remember when I mentioned intuition? That's your higher self whispering from the backseat!

As we start to remember who we really are, we begin listening to that backseat driver more. Gradually, this guidance becomes clearer and starts blending into our daily lives. Imagine your higher self moving up front, becoming your co-pilot—a wise best friend on this journey.

When we strengthen our bond with our higher self, we navigate life with more clarity and purpose. We learn to observe our thoughts without letting them control us, allowing us to live more authentically and align with our soul's true intentions. This connection allows us to make better decisions in alignment with our soul contract.

Roberto Assagioli (1888–1974) was an Italian psychiatrist and a pioneer in humanistic and transpersonal psychology. He introduced the concept of the higher self, believing that 'the Higher Self is an active centre. It activates and pulls the individual towards their development'.

SOUL CONTRACT

What is a soul contract? What if I told you that before we were born, we made agreements about the lessons and experiences we'd encounter? These are our soul contracts. This is why remembering who we are is crucial and why we want to have our co-pilot helping us along the way!

Sometimes, hitting a major junction in our soul contract can change everything. This happened to me with my bookkeeping business. A series of stumbling blocks led me to decide to sell the business. Each hurdle had the same message, but I wasn't listening. It took a bizarre situation—a bug stuck in my ear for over three hours during a trip to Queensland, Australia—to make me realise I needed to pay attention. While my hearing was blocked, my inner voice, my higher self, was not! It was very clear: '*Ear, listen, I'm not listening*'. Once I recognised the message, everything started to flow.

My right ear was the one affected, symbolising my struggle to listen to my current situation. After selling my business, I saw that ignoring those messages could have led to much worse issues down the line. I love this saying: '*The universe throws you a stone, then a brick. Then it drops a house on you to get your attention*'. Until I aligned my actions with my soul's contract, everything felt blocked. This realisation inspired me to write this book.

Selling my business has allowed me to reshape my life to fit my soul's authentic journey. It has created a new timeline, free from negative energy. My family immediately sensed this change and felt the benefits of my new presence.

LESSONS

Life brings us lessons to help us grow. Every decision impacts our journey, regardless of past lives. Earth offers a unique opportunity to fast-track our learning by experiencing concepts firsthand. Our most significant lesson is often compassion for others—connecting emotionally, listening without judgement, and speaking with kindness.

Understanding that everyone makes mistakes and striving to alleviate the suffering of others without expecting anything in return helps us grow and connect more deeply. This selflessness benefits ourselves as well as others. By looking out for one another, we foster a caring community.

Relationships with friends and family can be challenging. Although it's said we can choose our friends but not our family, in a spiritual sense, we choose our family before coming to Earth to learn specific lessons.

Sometimes, one person learns important lessons before another. It's vital to respect each individual's journey. Relationships can be complex. If people become toxic, it may be time to move on for everyone's well-being. Such situations can hinder growth and prevent us from moving forward. While we may have more to learn from this person, it is crucial to recognise when a relationship no longer serves our best interests and have the courage to let go, allowing both parties the opportunity to heal and grow. When it's time to walk away, we open the path to new experiences and connections. I know this is not an easy task for many and it is something worthy of careful consideration.

Each soul comes to Earth with unique lessons. Old souls may want to master self-love and self-compassion, while new souls might focus on developing compassion for others. The ultimate goal for many souls is to become an ascended master, a soul that has learned both forms of compassion. This is no easy feat as self-love is one of the hardest things to learn and apply.

KARMA

The concept of karma has its roots in ancient India. Karma is a cornerstone of Hinduism, Buddhism and Jainism. The Vedas, some of the oldest sacred texts of Hinduism, dating back to around 1500 BCE, laid the foundations of karma. The term 'karma' comes from the Sanskrit word 'kri', which means 'to do' or 'to act'. Karma symbolises the idea that our actions in this life and in past lives shape our future through the cycle of reincarnation, known as Samsara. Samsara is influenced by actions that follow dharma or moral order. In short, good actions lead to positive outcomes—moral, kind, and ethical choices. Positive karma brings benefits, like happiness, prosperity or a favourable rebirth. Conversely, negative karma results from harmful or unethical actions driven by ill will, leading to suffering, challenges or less auspicious rebirths. Negative actions cause problems. From these perspectives, karma guides ethics. It shapes personal and communal destinies based on one's deeds.

Various cultures and belief systems around the world incorporate the concept of karma or cause-and-effect, extending beyond its Eastern roots. It is often summarised by the phrase, *'What goes around comes around'*. In Buddhism, the intentions behind actions determine the nature of one's karma, affecting future happiness or suffering.

Jainism views karma as a substance that clings to the soul and influences its future lives. Ethical living and nonviolent practices are believed to bring freedom from karmic oppression.

Cause-and-effect ideologies also appear in Christian doctrine. For instance, Proverbs in the Bible says, *'Whoever sows sparingly will also reap sparingly, and whoever sows generously will also reap generously'*. This idea emphasises that actions have direct results and is often seen as a universal law.

We came to Earth to enjoy this wonderful planet. However, sometimes negative karma from past lives or our actions here can create obstacles. Clearing negative karma is essential, and we must be mindful of our interactions with each other. Being careful with one another helps avoid creating more.

What might this look like? An example could be recurring patterns or habits, such as persistent negative relationships or issues with money. Reflecting on why these patterns persist is crucial for personal growth. Identifying and addressing these patterns or habits is key to personal development and karmic resolution.

So, get curious about karma. Patterns and habits can be ways in which karma presents itself. Consider why these situations keep recurring and decide to change the pattern or habit.

Here's a simple example of how karma can unfold over lifetimes: In a past-life, a husband might have cared for his wife after she had an accident. This act of care created a karmic bond and possibly even a debt if it wasn't balanced out then.

Now, let's fast forward to their next life, where the roles are reversed. This time, they come back as mother and son, tackling a new challenge together. The son, grappling with an illness, needs constant care, yet it's their deep love that pushes them forward. Guided by the universal law of karma, they work to resolve their old karmic debt, supporting one another and drawing strength from their bond. Their shared love becomes the key to balancing the scales and healing old wounds.

SOULS AND THE HUMAN EXPERIENCE

When we chose to come to Earth, we knew we would not remember where we came from, as that was part of the agreement. Some souls have trouble integrating in this lifetime; they may not realise it, but subconsciously, they long to be with their soul family. Signs of this include a persistent sadness, a sense of longing for something else and difficulty forming friendships and relationships.

Now, more old souls are coming to this Earth to help raise the collective vibration and bring love and happiness to this world. Our souls were eager to come here; otherwise, we would not have come. We made many decisions before arriving on Earth. Yet, one constant for all humans is free will. This ability influences the decisions we make in this lifetime.

We must understand that we are here to learn about the polarity of the human experience—the contrasts between the bad and the good in life —and how we can transform negative situations into positive ones or neutralise them. This is the path of learning.

Acknowledging everything that happens to us in this lifetime can be challenging, particularly when trauma leaves deep scars which are hard to overcome. Our attitude plays an important role in how we recover and move forward. Self-compassion is vital in healing. This means being aware of our pain and suffering while being kind to ourselves. It is important to differentiate between self-compassion and self-pity. Feeling sorry for ourselves leads to negative emotions such as anger, hatred, rage and fear, which lowers our vibration and shifts our time-lines to a lower frequency, as mentioned in the 'Dimensions' chapter. This can sometimes seem like a difficult and complex world, but it is *what we do with it that matters most.*

Self-actualisation helps us gain clarity and transform our lives for the better. With self-compassion, we ask ourselves: *'What can I learn? What difference can I make? How can I recover from what has happened and find the strength to turn my challenge into the best version of myself?'* By inspiring us to overcome obstacles and move forward, we begin to see remarkable changes before our eyes, things that we never thought possible. Imagine reaching the higher frequency timeline and changing our lives. Many people who have experienced terrible events and hardship will tell you that it was this transformative thinking not only created change in their world but was also an integral pathway to peace and healing.

CHILDREN REMEMBERING WHO WE ARE

Babies and young children often have a clearer connection to where we have come from, lacking the amnesia that affects older individuals. As we grow older, we are taught many ways to conform. We learn that we are living in a fear-based society, and we all want to do what is accept-able in this society. Many people change because they want to forget who they actually are, as being different can be challenging without the love and support around us. Our beliefs and values are often instilled into us by our families and education system from a young age.

CAREFUL WISHES

Lao Tzu famously said, *'Watch your thoughts; they become your words. Watch your words; they become your actions. Watch your actions; they become your habits. Watch your habits; they become your character. Watch your character; it becomes your destiny'*. There is also a saying: *'Be careful what you wish for, lest it comes true!'* from Aesop's Fables.

I was having a conversation with someone, and they were telling me about their recent dentist visit. The dentist recommended a deep teeth cleaning. The dentist said this would help them a lot. Their reply to the dentist was, *'Well, I only have 4 to 5 years to live, so why pay that money to get my teeth done?'*

When they told me about this conversation, I was surprised because they were only seventy-six years old and in great health. I asked why they felt this way. Did they want dentures? Were they going to pass away at eighty years of age? I gently told them the more they repeated those words, the more they would manifest that reality. As soon as I explained to them what they were doing, they immediately took back the words. This connects with self-compassion.

Negative comments, even if they're made flippantly, can change our reality. It is the free will choice overtaking the actual soul contract. We must be conscious of our thoughts and ideas. You see the body and the universe respond; the body listens and doesn't understand flippant comments. When we're so flippant about what we say, we think it has no meaning, but if we say it too often, it starts to manifest in this life. We only want to manifest the life of the highest good. The other side is that we may be saying positive things, but our subconscious mind is doing the opposite. The subconscious needs time to adjust!

An example of this is whether to sell your house or not. You might consciously decide, *'Yes, I want to sell; this is what I want'*. Then you notice it's taking a long time to sell. So, you then need to start to ask questions. Do you really want to sell the house? Are you putting out subconscious thoughts to the universe that you don't want to sell? So, in our conscious mind, you know you want to sell, but perhaps you might be having some trouble letting go of the memories attached to the home.

HOW DO WE BECOME SUPERHUMAN?

Being *superhuman* means discovering our potential and exceeding perceived 'average human' capabilities. It involves remembering who we are and rebuilding ourselves with new beliefs and ideas. We all have the power to be superhuman; however, it takes work!

Adaptability

Adaptability is all about shifting your mindset. When you engage in adaptive thinking and take action, you can transform your life. Embrace new knowledge and concepts and keep an open mind to achieve this. A closed mind creates stagnant energy in the body. For example, at work, there may be new ideas and ways of doing things. You don't want them to change because, in your experience, the old way worked quite well. However, being open to others' ideas and progressions is crucial. Listen to others, and if their ideas resonate with you, give them a shot. Taking risks is an essential component of progress. Even if it doesn't pan out, you'll have gained valuable experience simply by trying. When we fear change, we prevent new possibilities from entering our lives!

Believing in Yourself

You can totally do this! The universe has your back. When you believe in yourself, you will gain more confidence. We all have unique strengths that are our superpowers. What are yours?

Revitalising Yourself

You can deplete your energy if you don't take care of yourself. Think of your energy as a renewable resource that requires maintenance, which means making time to meet your needs. Remember Maslow's Hierarchy? Make time for fun in your life and do the things you enjoy. Take time to rest and rejuvenate, take a break or engage in activities that bring you joy. It's great to be on the go, but it's important to know when to recharge. Revitalising is as essential as food and water. It provides sustenance! Once we're recharged, it's crucial to keep some energy in reserve so we don't deplete ourselves. Living a depleted life not only robs us of our dreams but also causes long-term negative effects. We can also miss opportunities because there is no space or mental energy to recognise them. Extra energy is a sure sign of super-human capabilities.

Getting Creative

When we adapt and store extra energy, we become excited about new projects or challenges. This stimulates the brain and can spark intense creativity as we imagine unique approaches. Viewing things from different perspectives can lead to original ideas and innovations. This approach makes life more engaging and opens your mind to new possibilities. Are you starting to see the symbiotic nature of these actions?

Managing Emotions

Learning new strategies that enhance your positive emotions and teach you how to regulate them is one of the greatest gifts you can give yourself. Knowing how to self-regulate and self-soothe is a superpower. If we don't know how to monitor and master our emotions, they can overwhelm us and dictate too much of our lives. Being able to manage emotions positively provides clarity in life and is yet another super-power. See the chapter on 'Emotions and Ailments' for a deeper dive into emotions.

Conscious Communication

We communicate in so many ways, and when we become more conscious and mindful in our interactions, it feels like we gain a super-power. When done well, it can truly enrich our lives.

Body language and tone are vital parts of our communication. Facial expressions, along with the tone of our voice, can communicate how we really feel without saying a single word. Gestures can add emphasis or send specific messages. Eye contact, for instance, shows you're paying attention, interested or feeling confident. Have you ever spoken to someone who is smiling, but the smile doesn't reach their eyes? We are intrinsically wired in many ways to feel a genuine connection, and we can sense it when it isn't there.

What about personal space? The distance we keep can communicate about how we feel—whether it's intimacy, aggression or formality. Touch, like a handshake or a friendly pat on the back, can show support or affection. And sometimes, silence speaks volumes; what we don't say can be just as important as what we do say.

When we're aware of how we interact on a deeper level, we can be more compassionate, and people tend to be more receptive to our intentions. It also helps us build thoughtful, growth-inspired connections.

So now that we have some ideas about the higher self and how to be superhuman, how do we truly connect with the essence of who we are?

THE ESSENCE OF THE PERSON

What does the true essence of a person mean? I believe the true essence of a person is the aura they present to the world. It's the feelings, emotions and energy they emit. It's their personal qualities and consciousness. Living with love and positivity allows wonderful things to shine through. This is the true you that the world sees. When we live with this intention, it allows others to see the real us!

Our deepest self understands our true nature, making us feel complete. It is our connection to the universe's energy that clarifies our consciousness and awakens our true self. We are a part of it.

HERE ARE WAYS TO REMEMBER WHO YOU ARE—THE ESSENCE OF YOU:

Place Your Hands on Your Heart

Take the time to rest, place your hands on your heart and feel the wonderful energy that is there. Close your eyes and sit or lie quietly, listening to what your heart is telling you. Who are you? Notice your feelings. Can you name those emotions? Is it excitement, joy, happiness, sadness or anger? Write them down in a journal so you do not forget.

Spend Time With People Who Have a Positive Energy

Surround yourself with positive-minded people who will fill your life with laughter and light. They may help you find out what you truly enjoy in life. They might even inspire you and give you the courage to really look at yourself. When we surround ourselves with positive people, we can experience a sense of calm and feel valued. And we can return the favour!

Practice Self-compassion

Sometimes, we can be tough on ourselves, especially when we make mistakes or notice things that we don't like about ourselves. While we may easily be able to show empathy and compassion for others, it can be much harder to show compassion for ourselves. Practising self-compassion means showing yourself the kindness you would give to others. How would you treat your child or best friend in this situation? This is what self-compassion looks like.

Be Spontaneous

Do things that help you find joy, even if they are last-minute decisions. Sometimes, you need to shake things up a bit and do what you want to do. When I think of spontaneity, I think about things that I do for fun. We may often go through life ruled by schedules, living step-by-step, minute-by-minute days. By being spontaneous, we step outside of the norms of our lives and live life to the fullest.

Living life to the fullest means living with no regrets. I can look at my life and say that I have no regrets. Everything that has happened in my life has had a reason, and I have learned from it all. I have never believed in self-pity, as that is not why we are here on this Earth. Of course, I get upset, cry or laugh if something happens. I still experience the emotions and challenges that life brings. But I have learned that every experience offers a lesson that can improve my life. I am enjoying living each day in the present, being mindful of everyone and everything that is around me. Live your best version, the best timeline of your life, because we never know where it will lead us. You might end up down the garden path, but even that has its own beauty.

Remembering who we are is the crucial ingredient on our path and helps us understand why things happen in our lives and how we can deal with them. It helps us recognise why this reality is always changing. It changes with our beliefs and ideas and with our perception of the life we want. We are souls having a human experience in this reality, knowing that there is much beyond this world to look forward to.

DIMENSIONS

 'Everything in the universe has a rhythm, everything dances'. — Maya Angelou

You have probably heard the word 'metaphysical'. The Oxford Dictionary defines the term as 'things that are beyond our perception and touch, such as the nature of existence and the cosmos'. So, how does this relate to dimensions? Recently, the term 'dimensions' has appeared in mainstream spiritual and scientific discourse.

When we talk about dimensions in everyday conversation, we usually refer to the depth, width and height of something. However, in the context of self-actualisation, we delve deeper into different measurements and aspects of reality. I am going to attempt to explain this simply, though it is not easy, as this is a very complex topic! In spiritual discourse, dimensions also refer to various planes of existence or states of consciousness.

Many scientists believe that our universe may not be the only one out there, and the study of these theories sparks great debate. These universes may potentially interact with ours in ways we haven't yet discovered. Exploring dimensions allows us to peek into these incredible possibilities.

Scientists can measure and observe our physical reality; they can study it. Spiritual reality, however, relates to our consciousness, our higher self and our soul. It is a world beyond the physical—a more extrasensory reality. It is much harder to study and is linked to our perception of human experiences. By 'dimensions', we are referring to the spiritual ones, not physical ones. While we share the same physical reality, our consciousness may perceive it differently.

At the moment, we are living in a physical reality that primarily consists of matter and energy. This includes the particles and forces that interact to create the observable universe. It is a much denser energy.

This is the third dimension. It is very limiting, and we can weigh ourselves down with fear, separation, tiredness and anxiety. Our ego can take centre stage when we base our self-worth on others' opinions. In this dimension, time and space define us, and we perceive things by width, height and depth.

When we raise our vibration, time becomes less constrictive, and our reality starts to change. This state is an in-between phase of awakening and doesn't last long. We are forging that alignment I mentioned earlier with our co-pilot—the higher self, our soul. As discussed in earlier chapters, we start to observe how we relate to the world around us.

Third Dimension (3D): In this dimension, our thoughts and beliefs are a major factor. We see ourselves as individual consciousness, not as one collective whole. This stage is characterised by individualism, materialism and ego, often leading to judgement and a lack of compassion for others and ourselves. Our world, as we see it, is in 3D.

Fourth Dimension (4D): In this dimension, we connect with our inner self, higher consciousness and intuition. Our awakening journey begins as our consciousness expands, allowing us to tap into the collective. We shift from a fear-based reality to one rooted in love. We purge negative emotions and beliefs, realising we are more than our physical bodies—we are emotional beings. We realise there is more to this world than meets the eye. The fourth dimension is also referred to as the astral plane.

Fifth Dimension (5D): In the fifth dimension, we experience unity consciousness, and we dwell in the heart space. Our human senses cannot perceive this dimension at all, as we cannot hear, see, feel or taste it. We exist fully in the moment, the now, nothing, without thoughts of the past or the future. Manifestation unfolds naturally in this dimension, and we are fearless. We feel endless gratitude and love as our ego fades away. We serve others out of love, not caring about material possessions or our status; we are happy to go with the flow. This is the causal plane, where we create our own perception of reality.

Sixth Dimension (6D): In the sixth dimension, we gain knowledge and wisdom that surpass human understanding.

Seventh Dimension (7D): In the seventh dimension, we experience oneness and enlightenment. It is the realm of love, perfection and unity where individual souls merge into one collective consciousness.

TIMELINES

Have you ever heard of timelines or multidimensional theory? I will try to keep this as simple as possible. Consider that every decision we make creates a new timeline. Take a simple choice: having a cup of coffee or not. These seemingly simple choices can split into two time-lines—one where you drink the coffee and one where you decide not to. Now imagine, throughout the day, every choice you make, like going for a walk or staying in, adds more branches. Each moment, our decisions create an infinite number of timelines. Some scientists even entertain the idea that the creation of a new timeline generates a whole other dimensional reality. Imagine that—millions of versions of you, living different lives with different experiences? This is more than a little mind-boggling.

What Timeline Are You Creating?

When you think about it, each decision aligns with a different version of your life. Some timelines reflect the best version of the life you want, while others may be more fear-based and negative. It's important to evaluate your choices, aiming to align them with your highest good. Unfortunately, feelings of fear or unworthiness can inadvertently actualise a lower vibrational timeline.

In the diagram at the end of this chapter, we can visualise how the decisions we make influence the timeline that we experience.

On this timeline, money, careers and relationships converge seamlessly with our desires. This is why manifesting with positive energy is crucial; it helps us claim the best version of our lives. I discuss this more in the chapters on 'Manifestation' and 'Reality'.

My invitation to you is to embrace the idea that when we explore our dimensional reality and consider possibilities beyond what we can see, touch or smell, the weight of our physical world starts to dissipate. We can move beyond this world when the transmutation of lower vibrations and blockages is stripped away. The reality we accept can be transcended, opening the door for us to marvel at the complexity and beauty of our awakened souls.

TIMELINES

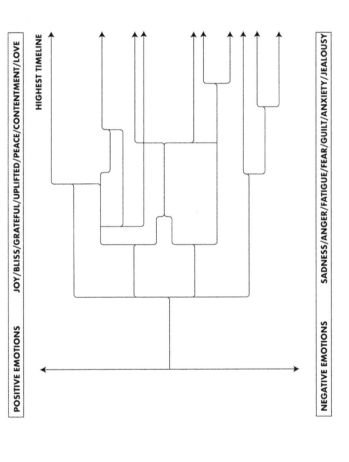

PART II
THE SPIRITUAL TOOLBOX

Welcome to Part Two: The Spiritual Toolbox.

We're about to explore some truly life-changing practices. Some you may have heard about and may already practise, and some will be new.

Think of these tools and methods as ingredients in a soul-nourishing recipe ready to be used in your unique way. Maybe you'll find clarity in your goals while sitting under a tree, or perhaps your next big idea will spark during a deep meditation session or while jotting down your dreams.

We'll look at the complex dance between emotions and physical illnesses, highlighting how our emotional health intimately relates to our physical health.

Have you ever experienced that flash of déjà vu that stopped you in your tracks? This could be the perfect moment to pause and spot an old habit you're finally ready to break free from. Maybe a quiet moment of mindfulness will fill you with gratitude, inspiring you to perform a random act of kindness or to better understand yourself and the parts of your ego that need some fine-tuning.

This section is all about learning and weaving these practices into your daily life to enrich your personal growth and self-actualisation.

CHAKRAS

'Within you, there is a stillness and a sanctuary to which you can retreat at any time and be yourself. The seven chakras are the wheels of this internal sanctuary, guiding you to peace and enlightenment'. — Hermann Hesse

Rooted in ancient Indian texts, including the Vedas, Upanishads and Patanjali's Yoga Sutras, chakras are centres through which energy flows and regulates consciousness in the brain. In yoga, they are activated by breath and postures (Marathe et al., 2020). Seven main chakras serve as integral components of the energy networks linking the body, mind and spirit.

Each chakra rotates at a different frequency, controlling our energy flow and influencing our spiritual, emotional and physical states. They facilitate the circulation of prana, or life force, through our body's energy pathways, called nadis, and spin at a particular frequency.

When our chakras are balanced and open, prana flows smoothly, maintaining our health and energy. Blockages or imbalances can disrupt the vitality of our chakras, affecting our physical, emotional or spiritual well-being.

The seven chakras are the Root Chakra, Sacral Chakra, Solar Plexus Chakra, Heart Chakra, Throat Chakra, Third Eye Chakra and Crown Chakra.

I strongly believe that when our thoughts are positive, our chakras are aligned, and the energy in our body is free-flowing. Wherever the mind goes, energy flows. Blocked chakras lead to depression, low energy, negative thoughts and emotions, tiredness and anxiety. Understanding our bodies and how our chakras function can help us lead more healthy and vibrant lives. According to Marathe et al. (2020), when a chakra is blocked, we may experience underactive or overactive chakras as they try to compensate for the inefficiency.

Bhetiwal (2017) further states that by balancing the chakras, the body can become more resilient to stress-related psychosomatic illnesses, such as irregular heart rate, high blood pressure, poor digestion, and other dysfunctions.

EACH CHAKRA IS REPRESENTED BY THE BELOW FEATURES:

Colour

Each of the seven chakras is represented by a different colour of the rainbow. Christopher Hills, a British-born author, scientist, and philosopher, is known for his contributions to the understanding of chakras in the Western world. In his 1977 book *Nuclear Evolution: Discovery of the Rainbow Body*, Hills elaborated on the idea of the association of the chakras with the colours of the rainbow, a concept that has been widely accepted worldwide.

Each colour emits its own unique wavelength of light, influencing both mood and perception. According to Bhetiwal (2017), the wavelengths of these colours correspond to specific Hz frequencies that our bodies vibrate to, aligning with each chakra.

Lotus Flower

The idea of chakras as lotus flowers comes from ancient Indian spiritual traditions, particularly Hinduism and Buddhism. These traditions use the lotus flower as a symbol of purity, enlightenment and spiritual growth. Ancient texts like the *Shat-Chakra-Nirupana* and the *Upanishads* describe these chakra flowers in great detail. Picture each chakra as a lotus flower with a specific number of petals. When these chakras are balanced, the petals are open and spread evenly, spinning gracefully like a colourful spinning top from our childhood.

Frequencies

Sound is a form of energy that travels through the air as waves of frequencies. Each chakra resonates with a particular frequency of sound, which can help open the chakra or clear dense energy. These frequencies are highly specific to each chakra.

Music is made up of many different frequencies, and some tracks include subliminal messages—words layered beneath sounds like rain or music, often in a meditation music track. These will be heard by your subconscious mind as they are in the background. It's important not to drive when listening to these.

Listening to different frequencies during meditation can enhance concentration and help restore balance to the chakras.

SOUND BOWLS

Another powerful modality used for chakra alignment and balancing is sound bowl healing. You might have heard of these as singing bowls due to the singing sound they make. Sound bowls are specifically designed to match the frequencies of our chakras, helping to tune and balance these energy centres. Various practitioners specialise in sound bowl therapy.

Sound bowls come in various sizes, qualities and shapes, each producing different tones that impact different parts of the body.

The tones are generated by striking a bowl with a mallet, causing the bowl to vibrate at a level that can relieve energy blockages in our chakras. This process can help reduce stress and any tension held within the body.

A study conducted by Goldsby et al. (2017) found that there was a significant improvement in participants' well-being when quartz crystals and Tibetan singing bowls were used. The participants experienced reduced mood tension, anxiety and pain and an overall increase in their spiritual well-being. Participants who had no previous knowledge about singing bowls experienced a greater reduction in pain than those who were familiar with them. Similarly, a randomised crossover study found that incorporating a Himalayan singing bowl into a directed relaxation session led to greater declines in systolic blood pressure and heart rate, enhancing both physiological and psychological responses (Landry, 2014).

EMOTIONS

Chakras are significantly impacted by our thoughts and emotions, as emotions hold frequency, too! Positive emotions like love, joy and confidence keep our chakras open, and energy flows smoothly throughout our system. Conversely, when we are consumed by negative emotions like fear, anger and insecurity, our frequency is denser. This can block our chakras, throwing them out of balance and causing havoc. When we vibrate at a higher frequency through positive thoughts and actively work through those negative emotions, we can keep our chakras healthy and improve our overall well-being.

ORGANS

Each major organ in our body is connected to a specific chakra. When our chakras are balanced, they ensure a smooth flow of positive energy to their corresponding organs.

PHYSICAL AILMENTS

Since chakras are aligned with major organs, physical symptoms can arise when they are blocked or congested. Common symptoms include dizziness, migraines, asthma, blood pressure, diabetes, nausea, constipation and exhaustion.

FOODS

The idea that what we eat can affect our chakras and overall well-being stems from both ancient wisdom and modern practices. Ayurveda, an ancient Indian system of medicine, teaches us that our diet plays a crucial role in balancing our body's energy. Modern holistic practices have embraced this idea, linking specific foods to each chakra based on their colour and nutritional benefits. In Hinduism, food is believed to carry life force energy (prana) that nourishes our entire energy system. We will cover more of this in the chapter 'Are We What We Eat?'

Chakra Position In The Body

Crown Chakra

Crown Chakra - Sahasrara	
Aspect	**Details**
Location	Top of head
Symbol	Pink lotus with 1000 petals
Frequency	963 Hz
Function	Connection with source, transformation
Imbalances/Blockages	Lack of purpose and focus, depression, distracted, confusion, limiting beliefs, attachments and disconnection
Physical Systems	Spinal cord, brainstem, pituitary gland
Ailments and Illnesses if Blocked	Migraine, chronic fatigue, headache, light sensitivity, learning issues
High Vibrational Foods	Blueberries, raspberries, grape juice, poppy seeds, blackberries, cauliflower, purple onions

Third Eye Chakra

Third Eye Chakra - Ajna	
Aspect	**Details**
Location	Between eyebrows
Symbol	Purple lotus with 2 petals
Frequency	852 Hz
Function	Intuition, spiritual communication, awareness, perception
Imbalances/Blockages	Fear, anxiety, depression, doubt
Physical Systems	Pineal gland, eyes, ears, nose, pituatry gland, brain, hypothalamus
Ailments and Illnesses if Blocked	Scalp issues, seizures, eye strain, sinus, memory issues, dizziness, migraines
High Vibrational Foods	Eggplant, purple grapes, blueberries, goji berries, raw cacao, garlic, honey

Throat Chakra

Throat Chakra - Vishuddha	
Aspect	**Details**
Location	Base of throat
Symbol	Blue lotus with 16 petals
Frequency	741 Hz
Function	Creativity, voice, emotion
Imbalances/Blockages	Inability to express thoughts and emotions such as fear and doubt
Physical Systems	Throat, thyroid gland, mouth, jaw, shoulders, neck
Ailments and Illnesses if Blocked	Thyroid issues, hearing issues, sore throat, gum disease, laryngitis, headaches, stiff neck, sore jaw
High Vibrational Foods	Apples, honey, lemons, coconut water, herbal tea, plums and pears

Heart Chakra

Heart Chakra - Anahata	
Aspect	**Details**
Location	Center of chest
Symbol	Green lotus with 12 petals
Frequency	639 Hz
Function	Compassion, joy, unconditional love
Imbalances/Blockages	Lack of self-love, heartache, jealousy, anger, abandonment
Physical Systems	Heart, chest, arms, hands, lungs
Ailments and Illnesses if Blocked	Upper back, shoulder, arm and wrist pain, heart disease, blood pressure, asthma, lung issues, breast issues, poor circulation, lymphatic issues
High Vibrational Foods	Broccoli, spinach, kale, lime, avocado, peas, kiwi, celery and cucumber

Solar Plexus Chakra

Solar Plexus Chakra - Manipura	
Aspect	**Details**
Location	Belly button
Symbol	Yellow lotus with 10 petals
Frequency	528 Hz
Function	Self-confidence, sense of power, gut feeling
Imbalances/Blockages	Stress, anger, powerlessness, life feels uncontrollable
Physical Systems	Pancreas, liver, bladder, nervous system, stomach, adrenal glands, lungs
Ailments and Illnesses if Blocked	Diabetes, stomach ulcers, pancreatitis, trauma, nausea, dizziness, insomnia
High Vibrational Foods	Lemons, mangoes, pineapple, ginger, fennel, squash and quinoa

Sacral Chakra

Sacral Chakra - Svadhisthana	
Aspect	**Details**
Location	Below belly button
Symbol	Orange lotus with 6 petals
Frequency	417 Hz
Function	Emotions, feelings, sensuality, creativity
Imbalances/Blockages	Mental and emotional overwhelm, guilt, shame, lack of interest in sex, creative blocks
Physical Systems	Female reproductive organs, spleen, kidneys, adrenal glands, appendix, bowel, stomach, upper intestines, autoimmune system
Ailments and Illnesses if Blocked	Lower back pain, urinary tract infections, impotence, ovarian cysts, appendix, kidney and reproductive issues
High Vibrational Foods	Oranges, carrots, mangos, apricots, and sweet potatoes

Root Chakra

Root Chakra - Muladhara	
Aspect	**Details**
Location	Base of spine
Symbol	Red lotus with 4 petals
Frequency	396 Hz
Function	Grounding, security, connection with Mother Earth
Imbalances/Blockages	Fear, insecurity, panic, low self-esteem, anxiety
Physical Systems	Male reproductive organs, immune system, legs, feet, rectum, tailbone
Ailments and Illnesses if Blocked	Constipation, sciatica, arthritis, sore knees, eating disorders, exhaustion
High Vibrational Foods	Strawberries, beetroot, potatoes and carrots

CLEANSE YOUR SPACE

 'Smile, breathe, and go slowly. Your home is your first sanctuary. Make it a place where you can relax and find peace'. — Thich Nhat Hanh

Have you ever noticed how hanging out with someone can leave you feeling supercharged or, on the flip side, totally drained? It's like we 'catch' the energy vibes they're giving off. When it's dense or heavy, it can really weigh us down, making us feel flat or even a bit down in the dumps.

Have you ever walked into a building full of old objects and felt a heavy atmosphere around you? It's as if the walls and those old items are holding onto years of energy, some of which can be quite dense. This kind of energy can impact how we feel, sometimes making the air seem thicker or our mood a bit gloomier. Conversely, spending time in high-vibrational, clean energy, like being in nature, feels uplifting!

WHAT ARE SOME SIGNS THERE IS NEGATIVE ENERGY IN OUR HOME OR SPACE?

- Unrest or arguments between people in the space
- Tiredness—low energy, feeling lazy
- Negative thoughts, bitterness, depression and difficulty having positive thoughts
- Clutter
- Unpleasant smells or bad odours
- Trouble sleeping or frequent nightmares
- Issues with money
- A general feeling that something doesn't feel right

HOW CAN WE CLEANSE OUR AREA?

Salt

Salt can be a powerful tool for cleansing our space. Mix it with warm water and wipe down surfaces that need cleansing *(making sure the surface is suitable for salt use).* Salt can also be placed in small bowls in various corners of the home or spread out along the front and back doorways. Leave there for a few days to absorb negative energy, then discard it.

Salt can also be used to cleanse ourselves. Mix it with water, apply the mixture while showering, and rinse it off or add it to a warm bath. The salt I prefer is Himalayan salt or pink salt, which has a high concentration of minerals and is perfect to use for cleansing.

Diffuser

Using diffusers with essential oils can be a great way to clear negative energy from our home or space. By adding a few drops of high-quality essential oil to water, a diffuser can purify our home's atmosphere effectively. It's important to choose premium oils, as lower-quality oils only enhance the scent without truly cleansing the space.

Essential Oils for Cleansing and Purifying:

- Lavender: known for its calming and relaxing properties, lavender oil can reduce stress and promote a peaceful atmosphere.
- Sage: much like its use in smudging, sage essential oil is effective for clearing negative energy and purifying the space.
- Frankincense: this oil is excellent for spiritual cleansing, creating a meditative environment, grounding oneself and connecting to higher consciousness.
- Palo Santo: famous for its uplifting properties, Palo Santo essential oil brings positivity and helps dispel negativity.
- Lemon oil: refreshing and energising, lemon oil clears away negative energy and brings clarity and focus.
- Eucalyptus: with strong purifying properties, eucalyptus oil clears the air of negative energy and promotes mental clarity.
- Peppermint: known for its refreshing scent, peppermint oil clears negative energy and boosts our mood and energy levels.
- Tea Tree: a powerful antiseptic and purifier, tea tree oil can help cleanse our space of negative energy and unwanted influences.
- Rosemary: this oil clears the mind and space of negative energy, promoting mental clarity and protection.
- Cedarwood: with grounding properties, cedarwood oil creates a protective barrier against negative energy, promoting a sense of security and calm.

Using these essential oils in a diffuser can help create a more positive, harmonious, and balanced environment in our home or space.

Incense for Smudging/Clearing:

Traditionally used for cleansing our space, material items, and even our physical body, white sage is used to remove any negative energy and offers protection.

Palo Santo is known for bringing positivity to the space. Palo Santo can be used after white sage to bring uplifting energy to the cleansed space. Ensure that the Palo Santo you purchase is ethically sourced.

How to Cleanse/Smudge the Home

Using incense sticks and white sage bundles can also be used for smudging/cleansing. Smudging regularly helps you clear the energy you bring home, whether good or bad, ensuring your environment stays clean and energetically balanced. While there is no best time to smudge, it can be done day or night. It is incredible to see how people's energy can change to a positive one when a place has been cleansed and our space feels lighter. Here is a step-by-step guide to cleanse/smudge:

1. Open windows and doors: Allow air to circulate around the space if possible. You only need some fresh air, not a draft.
2. Set an intention: Before you begin, set an intention to remove any negative energy from this space and only allow light and love to flow through. Say a prayer out loud or silently, an affirmation or a mantra; it is up to you.
3. Ignite the white sage or incense stick and let it burn briefly. Blow out the flame and let the smoke rise.
4. Walk around your space slowly, allowing the smoke to waft around the room. Hold the white sage over a heat-proof bowl or plate to catch the embers. Make sure you smudge the corners of the room and behind doors. If preferred, a feather can be used to guide the smoke in specific directions.
5. Cleanse items or yourself: Allow the smoke to waft around you and the item
6. Extinguish the white sage or incense stick: After you have finished smudging, fully extinguish the sage or incense so there is no longer any smoke billowing from it.
7. Let fresh air circulate: After you have cleansed your home or space, allow the fresh air to circulate a while longer throughout the space and then close all windows and doors.

Let There Be Light

Open the curtains and windows to let light and fresh air flow through the room. Using sunlight to clear or enhance energy in a room is a practice that dates to ancient times. Cultures like the Egyptians, Greeks and Romans valued sunlight for its purifying and life-giving properties.

Scientific benefits of sunlight: Sunlight boosts mood by increasing serotonin levels, which can reduce feelings of depression and anxiety. It also helps regulate our sleep-wake cycles, or circadian rhythms, ensuring better sleep quality along with enhancing our cognition. (Chellappa, Gordijn & Cajochen, 2011) Moreover, sunlight helps the body produce vitamin D in our skin, which supports bone health and immune function. The UV rays from the sun have natural disinfecting properties, killing bacteria, viruses and mould spores, which helps keep indoor environments cleaner and healthier. (Holick, 2004)

Enhancing energy with sunlight: Natural sunlight also enhances the positive energy in a space. When sunlight floods a room, it creates a warm and inviting atmosphere that helps dispel negative energy, making the environment feel more uplifting and harmonious. In modern homes, large windows and open spaces are often designed to let in as much natural light as possible. Simple practices like opening windows, drawing back curtains and arranging furniture to catch sunlight can make a big difference. This not only creates a brighter, more inviting atmosphere but also promotes overall well-being.

How to Cleanse with Sound

Sound is also an effective way to cleanse negative energy from a room. The frequency 417 Hz is used, whether it be with bells, wind chimes, Tibetan singing bowls, music, clapping hands or even your favourite musical instrument.

The 417 Hz frequency is the same as the Sacral Chakra frequency, which can cleanse the room and help balance the chakra. I regularly use it to clear negative energy from our space.

Energy waves produce varying wave patterns depending on the frequency. The faster the movement, the higher the frequency and the higher the energy (Pūtaiao, P.A., 2018).

Crystals

Crystals hold surprising energy, and their use for healing and energy work has deep roots in ancient civilisations such as Egypt, Greece, Rome, China, India and Native American cultures. Modern practices draw on these ancient traditions, incorporating a blend of historical beliefs with contemporary metaphysical principles.

- Selenite: one of the most powerful cleansing crystals, selenite can clear negative energy from our homes and other crystals. Place selenite wands or slabs in the corners of the home to maintain a positive environment.
- Black Tourmaline: this stone grounds and protects against negative energy. Place black tourmaline near entryways to keep negative energy out and allow positive energy to flow in.
- Clear Quartz: known as the 'master healer', clear quartz can amplify both energy and intentions. Place clear quartz in different areas of your home to boost the energy and clarity of your space.
- Amethyst: this crystal helps to clear anxiety and stress while enhancing intuition. Keep amethyst clusters or geodes in living areas or bedrooms to promote a calm and peaceful atmosphere.
- Rose Quartz: known as the stone of love and compassion, rose quartz attracts love and promotes self-love. Place rose quartz in the bedroom or living space to foster a loving environment.
- Citrine: known for its ability to attract abundance and prosperity, citrine can be placed in areas where finances are handled, like the home office, to invite positive financial energy.
- Hematite: this grounding stone can help you stay focused and

confident. Place hematite in areas where you work or study to enhance productivity and creativity.

By incorporating these crystals into the home, you can create a space that is cleansed of negative energy and filled with positive, harmonious vibrations.

DECLUTTER YOUR HOME

Eckhart Tolle famously said, *'A cluttered space reflects a cluttered mind. Clear the clutter, clear the mind'*. We store not only emotional baggage in our bodies but also in our homes. When faced with the task of decluttering a room or a garage, it might seem overwhelming. We do not realise that there is emotion attached to all our material things as well, and we must learn to remove them when they are no longer needed. This can help us physically unload the emotions and help our minds have clarity as well.

Look around your home, the furniture and the decorations that you have. How do you feel when you look at them? Are they gifts that were given to you that you do not really like but are keeping things out of guilt? A way to help you decide on an item whether to keep it or let it go is, for example, if you have a vase, hold it in your hands. How does the vase make you feel? If you do not feel right or notice your energy dissipate, then it is time to let go of the item.

SOME WAYS YOU CAN DECLUTTER YOUR HOME

Rubbish

If there is rubbish, it is cluttering your house. This pile will weigh you down the most as this is the one that should have been let go a long time ago. Once a bag is full, throw it out. You will feel much better once you start. If anything is broken or missing parts, throw it out. You will never use it. You need to be strong, and you can do this.

Donate to Charity

Donating items that are still in good condition but are no longer needed will make you feel good as you are helping others in need. Remember, there are people in different stages of their lives who need assistance. If you find a charity to which you would like to donate your extra goods, then do it.

Keep

Now, be careful here. When keeping your goods, do not include anything that you will not use or that is of no value to you. You might think everything is valuable, but here is a short list of things to keep:

- **Photos**
- **Important documents**—read all papers thoroughly. Even if you make a pile to look at later, check them carefully to ensure you don't discard anything of value.
- **Items of sentimental or monetary value**—some things may appear to be rubbish at first glance, but make sure to check if they are family heirlooms or hold personal significance. Your family will not be impressed if you throw out something valuable!

Sell

The selling pile can help you earn some extra cash. You might consider selling your second-hand items online or at a garage sale. Ensure that the items are in good condition; otherwise, it may be better to add them to the rubbish pile.

Start with a Drawer

Decluttering can sometimes feel overwhelming. To make it more manageable, start with a single drawer or cupboard. You might start with your clothes. There's no right or wrong way to declutter. It's just about getting started without letting the task overwhelm you. If you feel that sorting through the wardrobe is enough for one day, that's perfectly fine. You can always return to finish the rest of the room later.

To reduce feelings of overwhelm, split the room into sections. I cannot stress enough the importance of completing the job. Remember, you will feel so much better and so much lighter.

Cleaning and clearing your home—and yourself—of negative energy involves more than just physical tidiness; it's about creating a sanctuary that nurtures your well-being and peace of mind.

Each method offers unique benefits, and certain practices may resonate more with you than others. Trust your intuition and choose the techniques that feel right for your home and personal energy. Embrace these rituals as acts of self-care and enjoy the renewal and balance they bring to your space.

Our home is our refuge. Regularly clearing negative energy helps maintain a harmonious and vibrant atmosphere, making it easier for us to relax, recharge and thrive. By doing so, we actively create an environment that supports our health, happiness and spiritual growth.

Ultimately, the goal is to cultivate a living environment that reflects and supports the best version of yourself. Happy cleansing!

GRATITUDE

 'Gratitude is not only the greatest of virtues, but the parent of all the others'. — Cicero

Gratitude is a warm feeling of appreciation and thankfulness that fills our hearts when we recognise the goodness in our lives.

Many of us may go through life unaware of the beauty and blessings around us, missing opportunities to feel grateful. However, we can make gratitude a daily practise. A review published by the University of New England, Australia, titled 'The Association Between Gratitude and Depression: A Meta-Analysis' (Iodice et al., 2021), found that people with higher levels of gratitude reported greater optimism, positive emotions and life satisfaction. Those who practise gratitude often also have higher self-esteem and view themselves more positively. The review also explained that over 264 million people worldwide suffer from depression and found that the more gratitude people practised, the less depressed they were. Gratitude is a simple strategy that can serve as an additional tool when managing anxiety and depression, and it helps to reduce negative thought patterns.

Another review by Wood et al. (2010) demonstrated significant improvements in well-being when participants practised gratitude. The review suggested that gratitude should be promoted as a practice widely, perhaps even on a national scale, as a powerful tool in positive psychology. The takeaway? Gratitude is not just a feel-good emotion; it is good for our health!

Recently, my husband and I visited Monument Valley in Utah, USA, with friends. We experienced an extraordinary tour that moved not only us but also our tour guide. This experience enriched our lives, and the soul and beauty of the place were beyond words—a time that I will never forget.

I took photos with the intention of capturing the moment. As I snapped each picture, I connected with my heart, the surroundings, and the people I was with. Looking back at the photos, I can relive those feelings.

It is important not to get caught up in the social media photo loop, taking pictures just for the sake of it to check off a list. While a check-list can be useful, we should be mindful, present and grateful for the opportunity to experience them. Too much phone time can steal our chance to be in the moment, too!

TAKE THE TIME TO EXPERIENCE LIFE

This was a magical, life-changing moment for us, witnessing that part of the world and the beauty there. We acknowledged the time and effort leading up to the trip and our arrival at the pre-planned destination. We did not let the adventure just fly past us with no recall; we allowed all the emotions and feelings to immerse us.

Gratitude can be enhanced by making time for everyday beauty, like watching a sunrise or sunset or watching the sky light up in full glory. One day, the sky may be filled with shades of pink, blue and orange and then it may be completely different the next. The sky is a chameleon of colour, offering moments to appreciate, pause and reflect.

ALLEVIATE STRESS

Our bodies do not handle stress well, yet we all experience it at some point. When stressed, we might notice our heart beating faster, our blood circulating more rapidly and a surge of adrenaline. Stress triggers the fight-or-flight response in our nervous system. However, if we become stressed for reasons unrelated to immediate danger, how do we reduce it?

Breathing exercises and physical activity can help. When stress begins to build, please take a moment to acknowledge its cause. One effective strategy is to be grateful for the awareness of the emotion and then let it go. It may seem unusual to pair 'stress' with 'gratitude', but our body is signalling that something needs attention. It is reacting to a perceived threat based on past experiences or recognition of danger.

Research by Toussaint et al. (2021) suggests that multiple forms of relaxation training—including progressive muscle relaxation, meditation, breathing exercises and visualisation—are beneficial. These methods can help reduce stress, enhance relaxation states and improve overall well-being. Over the past decade, a significant amount of research on gratitude has been undertaken by Dr Robert A. Emmons of the University of California and Dr Michael E. McCullough of the University of Miami. In one notable study, participants were asked to write a few sentences each week on specific topics. One group focused on things they were grateful for, while a second group documented daily irritations or disappointments. The third group wrote about events that had impacted them without distinguishing between positive and negative experiences. After ten weeks, those who expressed gratitude reported higher levels of optimism and greater life satisfaction. Interestingly, they also exercised more regularly and made fewer visits to physicians compared to those who concentrated on negative aspects of their daily lives.

In practising gratitude, we take time to review our situations and identify potential changes. In the section *How to Practise Gratitude*, I
describe some strategies I use when feeling stressed. These practices
can help you manage stress more effectively and bring more peace into
your life. Please remember to seek professional mental health advice
from a qualified practitioner if you are feeling unwell.

A BETTER NIGHT'S SLEEP

Everyone wants a good night's sleep. Everyone needs a good night's
sleep. Guess what? Gratitude can be a sleeping aid! It truly is the gift
that keeps on giving. If you have trouble sleeping, try expressing gratitude just before bed. Positive thinking before sleep, coupled with good
nutrition and exercise, can improve our rest. In a study by Wood et al.
(2009), researchers investigated whether individual differences in gratitude relate to sleep quality after controlling for neuroticism and other
traits. They found that gratitude predicted better subjective sleep
quality and longer sleep duration, along with shorter sleep latency and
reduced daytime dysfunction. The relationship between gratitude and
these sleep variables was mediated by more positive and fewer negative pre-sleep thoughts. Importantly, these results were independent of
the Big Five personality traits, including neuroticism and social desir-
ability.

Getting into the gratitude zone before bed helps you unwind and drift
into a restful slumber.

GIVE GRATITUDE WHEN EATING

Eating food, whether in a restaurant, at home or at work, should be an
experience, not a chore. We can make this enjoyable by taking a
moment to appreciate what is in front of us, savouring each morsel of
food as if it were our last, rather than consuming it without a thought.
Sometimes, when we eat, we don't fully realise we've done so because
we're not really paying attention. We might look at our plate and think,

'Did I just eat that?' We often overlook how it tasted: Was it spicy? Was it sweet? We could be enjoying our favourite pasta yet barely notice the flavours. It's as though we're eating cardboard instead of the delicious meal we've been looking forward to all day. We forget about the mix of ingredients, the flavours, the textures and the effort that went into preparing it. The food we eat is rich in details, and it's amazing that we get to experience this as humans.

OVERCOMING OBSTACLES TO GRATITUDE

This list is non-exhaustive; there may very well be areas of the world or your life that are not represented here, and that is okay. If that is the case, move on to practising gratitude in the next section.

Not Enough Time

It can feel like we never have enough time, and *'Learning meditation takes too long'* is the perfect excuse. Rush, rush, rush is what we do. The world constantly signals that we must keep moving and keep achieving. But in this mad dash, we lose sight of the small, precious moments that could bring us joy and gratitude.

Gratitude doesn't demand hours of your time. It thrives in brief, sincere moments. By slowing down and taking intentional breaks, we allow joy and beauty to seep into our lives. Suddenly, the mundane becomes meaningful. Balance is as simple as it sounds.

Too Tired

Gratitude only takes moments, and with practise, it becomes a wonderful habit. Exhaustion is a symptom of the modern world. Maybe we are overworked, tired of looking after children, tired of looking after the parents, tired of cooking and cleaning, tired of taking the train to work, tired of the long work hours, tired of being there for everybody and so on. The more we list, the more exhausted and over-whelmed we feel. You might even feel exhausted after just reading those sentences! At times, it feels like a heavy weight is keeping us down. But, suppose we turn this around and find energy and feel invigorated. We must start to show gratitude, even in small moments, such as appreciating the taste of that piece of fruit that we are eating.

Comparing Ourselves to Others

When my twins were nine years old, and my eldest was eleven, they came home from school one day and asked me why I did not always buy toys and whatever they wanted whenever we went to the shops. They said their friends always had the latest clothes and toys, and they wanted them as well. I asked them if they enjoyed the holidays we took, as we had started going on holidays for some quality family time. All these different adventures were intentional goals and took a lot of planning and saving to achieve. They all agreed they loved the holidays. I said to them that I would give them a choice of what they wanted, as we could not afford to do everything. However, if they wanted all the latest gadgets and clothes, then we would have to forgo our annual holidays.

They thought about this and agreed they wanted to go away more than have the latest things. They even appreciated everything, as the holidays were the best time we spent together. I must say I was very proud of my children.

I was lucky that my children chose to come to me, share what was on their minds and discuss any issues. They had been comparing themselves to their peers and did not want to be different, even though they were fortunate to have holidays. Their understanding that we can choose what we want and that it is okay to be different helped them detach from the need to be the same as others.

Bad Habits and Outdated Beliefs

Habit forming can be positive! It begins with a simple decision: committing to a practice that takes hold over time. When a habit is forged in positivity, we can profoundly alter our perspective and well-being. The real impact lies in the consistent actions we take. Actioning change is what we need. As Noel Dejesus said, *'Thoughts are free, talk is cheap, and action is expensive...'* Taking action requires effort, resources and sometimes risk. It is the most challenging part of the process but also the most valuable and impactful.

Releasing outdated beliefs that prevent us from feeling gratitude is crucial. If any of these reasons are stopping us, then it is even more reason to show gratitude, as we must change our beliefs and habits. Our beliefs are what make us the people we are, and if they do not align with the person we are or want to be, it is time to make the conscious choice to change.

NEGATIVE MINDSET

We must change our mindset to a grateful one by focusing on opportunities that present themselves and one of positivity rather than fear and negativity. If we cannot find gratitude in anything, then we need to ask ourselves why.

Below Are Some Aspects of the Human Condition That Stimulate a Negative Mindset:

- **Greed**: The desire to have more and more, with the belief that accumulating more will lead to greater happiness. This mindset often causes us to overlook the things we already have and should be grateful for.
- **Pride**: Pride can be positive, such as feeling proud of a promotion or completing a degree. However, when pride turns into arrogance, it becomes damaging. It can make it more difficult to be liked by others, leading to isolation.
- **Envy**: Wanting what another person has—whether it's their material possessions, achievements, skills or qualities—can cause us to overlook the desirable aspects of our own lives.
- **Narcissism**: Feeling superior to others does not serve us; it damages relationships with loved ones and hinders the development of new ones. A sense of entitlement can block genuine gratitude from emerging.

- **Pressure**: Thoughts and feelings of being overwhelmed and under pressure can build up over time. Finding small things to be grateful for each day can help us manage these difficult times.

Gratitude helps us grow, and it helps us awaken consciously. It must be authentic. If we are saying thanks just for the sake of it or to please others, we are not being truthful. It must be heartfelt, and it must mean something to us. Others can see when we are truly saying thanks to merely following social expectations. Change can only happen when it is sincere.

HOW CAN YOU PRACTISE GRATITUDE?

Below, there is a list of ways we can practise gratitude. These do not all need to be completed at the same time. Simply pick one or more that resonates with you and can be practised regularly. We want to develop a habitual practice of gratitude, so it becomes second nature. The more that any method is repeated, the easier it becomes.

Think of Five Things Each Day to Be Grateful For

Even if our day has been awful, there will be at least five things that we can choose to show gratitude for. These five things don't necessarily need to be directed towards another person; they can be 100 per cent internalised expressions. Examples of gratitude could be appreciating going for a walk, knowing that our family is healthy, spending a day with our friends, finding the time to engage in a hobby or going shopping. All we must do is express what we are grateful for. It's that simple. The more often we do this, the easier it becomes. This will help attract more of these positive experiences into our lives. I do this every night, but I also do this when I am having fun. Having an appreciation for what is happening is also an expression of gratitude. We might even have an a-ha moment when a new understanding comes to light or a lesson is learned; these are also reasons to express gratitude. *Being thankful is being full of thanks.*

Write Down Three Things That You Are Grateful For and Why They are Worth the Mention

We can take this one step further and write down three things we are grateful for and why we believe these are worthy of our attention, as this has many benefits. Not only does the act of writing help us to consciously think about what words we are writing down, but it also helps our minds to slow down and reflect. When we write, our subconscious mind listens to it! (Pennebaker, J. et al., 2011). Sometimes, when we are simply thinking about these things, we might be inclined to rush through our gratitude list in our minds. It is up to us to decide what works best for us. Notice I mentioned practise, as this should be done each day. We can make a gratitude journal and write down the three things in our journal each day. Consistency is important. Over days, weeks, or even years, we will be able to see how our gratitude has evolved and identify recurring themes. We may recognise a pattern that signals a need for change or reinforces that we are on the right path.

Saying Thank You to People

Saying thank you or showing appreciation to our fellow humans is another form of practising gratitude. This isn't when we feel obliged or should show appreciation; it is when we want to. Please do not assume that the other person knows that we appreciate what they have done. Others may have supported us through a situation, helped us when we needed help or they are just always there for us. Have we thanked them?

Some meaningful ways to express thanks include saying, 'Thank you so much for...', 'You are the best...', 'I cannot thank you enough for...', and 'I couldn't have done it without you'. Whether expected or not, this simple act of saying 'Thank you' can make someone's day, putting a spring in their step and showing that they are appreciated.

To show further gratitude, we can return the favour with the next step: *listening to people.*

Listen to People

Listening can be hard, and avoiding interruptions can be difficult, too. With the constant internal dialogue, it can be tricky to focus on being in a mindful state while we talk. It is so easy to think about what we will say next. It is meaningful when we actively listen to what another person is saying. Really tuning into what someone is saying is crucial to effective communication. This is called active listening. Active listening is such a game-changer! It really boosts our connections and shows appreciation for our relationships. Studies show that when we actively listen, we build empathy, trust and a deeper understanding of each other, making our bonds stronger. By being fully present and open, we create a safe space for others to share their thoughts and feelings. This helps them feel heard and valued, which is so important! (Jones, S. et al., 2019)

This also means not picking up our phone while someone is in the middle of a conversation because a message has just come through. We may not even realise we are doing this. How grateful would we be, and how grateful would the person we are sharing time with be, when we are both present and listening to each other in the conversation?

Giving a Compliment

Compliments can be given flippantly, but when sincere, they can truly make someone's day. Appreciation is showing gratitude. If I've just had a fantastic meal at a restaurant, I might compliment the chef on the incredible food. The person putting my groceries into shopping bags at the supermarket may have been very careful in packing all my items, showing consideration. I might take the opportunity to notice this and express my gratitude. When we pause, breathe and be present we allow ourselves to see and experience things to be grateful for.

Giving a Gift

Gift-giving is as old as time. In certain circumstances, we may decide to show gratitude by gifting a present to someone to say thank you. It does not need to be for an occasion; it can just be a gift because we want to give something. It does not need to be expensive; it could be a card. I know that it may feel awkward to us, but writing the card can help us put our thoughts and emotions down on paper so that in the future, the note or card can be looked at again and again. Remember, what we write on the card can be the biggest gift of all.

Examples of Gifts You Can Give:

- Setting aside an hour to go bike riding with your son/daughter/friend
- Helping to clean up the dishes after dinner
- Gifting someone their favourite book
- Visiting your elderly neighbour on your street

Examples of What You Can Add to a Card:

- *I wanted to thank you for listening to me the other day, as that made me feel so much better.*
- *I just wanted to let you know that you are such a good friend, as you are always there for me in times of need.*
- *I appreciate everything that you do for me.*

Giving Back

Donating or giving back to help others is another way of showing gratitude. We can give back by donating our time, food, clothes, services and money. Choosing a charity that holds meaning for us and donating is a great way to give back and show gratitude for what the charity is trying to achieve. The joy and satisfaction that we feel when we are doing some good in the world is both a reward and an expression of gratitude. Every year, I select a few charities that I resonate with and donate to them. Some donations will be monetary, and if that is the case, then I do some research about how the money will be spent and how the charity is making a difference. In other cases, I will give clothes and things that we do not use anymore to charity, as there are always people who can greatly benefit from what we may not be using.

Smiling at People

A smile is worth a thousand words. This small gesture is worth so much, as the person on the receiving end feels appreciated. Smiling, even to strangers, gives them a reason to smile back. This is such a simple exercise and does not cost a thing. A great habit that we can form is taking a few seconds to smile at someone we frequently see, such as the barista at our local coffee shop.

A Hug

A hug can easily change a person's mood. Now, I am not saying to run outside in the street with a FREE HUG FOR EVERYONE sign, but I am saying that we can hug our family and friends for no reason at all. They may give us a weird look if we do not normally hug them, but when we get into this habit, it shows that we appreciate them, which is a form of showing love.

Appreciation Jar

Cut up paper into business card sizes. Have a pen or pencil ready and attach it to the jar that can be removed to write and then reattach, so there is always a pen handy. Every day, we can write a note about something we appreciate and put it in the jar. If we are feeling down or have negative thoughts and emotions, we can go to the jar and review all the things that we have been grateful for.

Some Examples of Notes That You Can Write to Put in the Jar Are:

- Moments that made you laugh: *'Today Paul put his jumper on backwards and was stuck. He had us all in stitches'*, and *'Sam said that Grandma lost her glasses today, and she was looking everywhere, but they were on the top of her head'*. It is that simple.
- I was so lucky today that I was able to go for a walk in the sunshine.
- I was able to catch the first train today and got a seat.

- I read a chapter in the book *Reality and Beyond This World,* and I was enthralled.

Respect Each Other

Respect isn't always associated with the practice of showing gratitude, but it is a powerful way to express it. We may not always realise when we are not showing respect to others. When we are catching up with a friend or family member, eating or having a drink with them, we can show respect and gratitude to that person by listening to them. This is using those active listening skills I mentioned earlier. Putting our phones down and joining the conversation is a good start, as there will be time afterwards to check the phone. We can notice emotions when they are talking—are they smiling, laughing, sad, crying or angry?

Respect is also shown by being thankful when someone is helping us, listening to us and being there whenever we need them. If respect is only a one-way street, it means we are receiving it, but not giving it. This suggests that ego, selfishness and disrespect have taken over.

Life cannot only be about us singularly; it must be about all of us. We find comfort when we have people supporting us when we need them most, but are we truly there for our family and friends when they need us? Remember earlier in the book where I mentioned that what you put out comes back? Gratitude and respect work the same way.

There are so many ways to show gratitude. By taking the time and making the most of opportunities to show gratitude, we remove ourselves from limitations that bring us down. We align ourselves with a happier and more positive version of ourselves. Gratitude helps us to live life to the fullest in the best possible way.

MEDITATION

 **'Peace comes from within. Do not seek it without'. —
Buddha**

Meditation and our reality: what does one have to do with the other?
When we allow time to experience a peaceful mind, we create a space
that stimulates our vision, and we instinctively know what course of
action to take.

BENEFITS OF MEDITATION

According to Sharma H. (2015), 'During the process of meditation,
accumulated stresses are removed, energy is increased and health is
positively affected overall. Research has confirmed a myriad of health
benefits associated with the practise of meditation'.

Some of the benefits mentioned in this article are:

- Stress reduction
- Decreased anxiety
- Decreased depression

- Reduction in pain (both physical and psychological)
- Improved memory and increased efficiency
- Reduced blood pressure and heart rate
- Reduced cortisol and epinephrine levels
- Increased melatonin levels

Meditation in any form is a great practice to bring into your day. It helps unite the body and spirit. For some, it can be a spiritual experience and an overall improvement in their well-being; others might only seek the health benefits. Note that I have started by saying practise, which is a crucial distinction to make. It doesn't matter what type of meditation you choose if you try to practise it every day, even if it is for short bursts; it is the key that will help you.

Meditation changes our lives. It helps us centre ourselves and is an amazing way to relieve our minds of too many thoughts. Many people will say they cannot meditate. So, I invite you to release any expectations. When there are no expectations, the most surprising things can happen. By meditating, we are giving ourselves the time and space to see the world and answer some of our questions. It permits us to look within as we allow the time and space for soul searching and enrichment.

For some, myself included, I thought meditation was too difficult and time-consuming, but once I learned to embrace it, even a five-minute meditation can give me clarity. Meditating for short spurts can inspire us, bring calmness to our lives that we may not have had previously and grow trust in ourselves that the decisions we are making are the correct ones. Once we get used to our five-minute meditation, we may seek other longer meditations that can help us transform our lives. I must admit it did take me a while to understand the whole concept of meditation. Every time I put the music on, I fell asleep, and the meditation was over. I thought, *'This doesn't work for me; how can I fall asleep every time?'* I then reviewed the way I was meditating, and afternoons or evenings were not working for me as my body would think I was having an afternoon nap or it was bedtime. Upon waking, I would complete a ten-minute meditation, or if I walked the dog in the morning, I would admire my surroundings, the sun and the clouds, and see the beauty of the day. This was my way of meditating, as it allowed me to be in the present. I still do this, and it's great for the mind and body.

Suppose we choose to meditate by walking, running or doing some exercise we love. In that case, this is soothing to our soul as we enjoy what we are doing, and we are giving our mind space to just be. I know that is hard to digest when we are trying to climb that hill and breathing hard; we think, *'Am I just being in the now?'* The answer is yes, you are. Giving ourselves the time to do the things we enjoy is a form of meditation.

Some people find cooking a form of meditation, as it is relaxing to measure the ingredients, prepare the meal, and then cook it. Others prefer to garden, watching plants grow from seedlings sown in the ground to fruit or vegetables or even large trees. This is a wonderful double-up in healing. In the chapter on 'Nature', you will find out that the great healer and stress reliever is right under your nose.

Meditation can reduce stress as we learn to focus on breathing and calm our minds. It helps us increase focus, improve our mood, improve cognition, improve pain issues and reduce inflammation (Sharma, 2015). We begin to experience the tingling beginnings of a sense of inner peace.

Hölzel et al. (2011) found that practising mindfulness-based stress reduction programmes such as meditation increases grey matter concentration over an eight-week study period. These changes affected the regions where the learning and memory processes, emotion regulation and self-referential processing occur.

When we start meditating, it can be very powerful, as we may release beliefs and emotions that are limiting us. This may heighten our sensitivity, and we can become emotional and teary. It is hard to persist if this is happening to us, but we are making a huge breakthrough, and this is all about the healing process for our bodies and minds. Perseverance is the key to making change.

Intentions

Meditation and intentions go hand in hand as they help create the tunnel to focus on something in particular; otherwise, our minds can drift too quickly. Past lives can be an intention, and we look at past lives in 'Remembering Who We Are' along with 'Timelines'. Meditation is a great space to do this if you would like to meet your higher self to ask a question.

Other intentions can also be set, such as manifesting what we desire. Pick one thing at a time to meditate on so you are giving it your utmost attention to bring it into this timeline.

MEDITATION TECHNIQUES

According to the article by Sharma H. (2015), these are the five steps of meditation:

1. **Intention:** Set the intention of what you want to achieve from this mediation.
2. **Concentration:** Now, concentrate on this intention.
3. **Insight:** Focus on what you are experiencing. Are there any sensations?
4. **Sensitivity:** Here, you can feel tingling in parts of the body, lightheadedness, body twitching and involuntary moments.
5. **Release:** Release any negative emotions or feelings.

Basic Meditation

1. Find a quiet place.
2. Sit or lie down in a comfortable position.
3. Relax your body and close your eyes.

4. Take deep breaths to the count of four, expanding your stomach, which engages your diaphragm. Hold the breath for the count of four, and then push out the breath through your mouth to the count of six. Repeat this three times, and then breathe normally. Please ensure you only breathe at a rate that is comfortable for you.
5. Be aware if your mind has started to wander.
6. Bring your mind back to nothing; chanting may help you stay focused.
7. When you are ready to finish, bring your mind slowly back to the present and take some deep breaths.
8. When ready, open your eyes and take in what you feel or see during the meditation.

I am often asked when the best time is to meditate, and there is no right answer, as it must suit the person and their lifestyle. Meditation, whether it be walking, sitting or lying down, is best done when we find the time that we are the most comfortable.

Morning Meditation

Meditating in the morning is a great way to start the day in a positive mood, and it can set us up for the rest of the day. It is time spent on you, not anybody else. If you can get up a bit earlier than the rest of your household, you have that 'me' time that no one can break.

You can choose any meditation you feel is right for you. Sometimes, people tell me they aren't in the mood to meditate, but if meditation can change our mood, then it is worth considering.

Evening Meditation

Some benefits of meditating before bed are that your mind can relax from the busyness of the day and detach from any stress or pressure you may have felt. This may lead to an increase in melatonin, a decrease in your blood pressure and a reduction in insomnia or sleep issues.

If you want to practise meditating on your own, commence with five minutes, then ten minutes, and then fifteen minutes. You can meditate for longer if you prefer. Also, try to eliminate coffee at night before bed and avoid going to bed with a full stomach. Even though I have added these forms of meditation to bedtime, they can be practised in the morning if that suits you better.

TO GET YOU STARTED, BELOW ARE SOME WAYS YOU CAN MEDITATE BEFORE BEDTIME:

Ask Three Questions Before Bed

A friend told me about their nighttime routine: They asked three simple questions when they went to bed. They hadn't realised they were still practising a form of meditation. This is what they did:

Lie down, ready to go to sleep. Close your eyes, take three full deep breaths, then breathe normally and ask these three questions:

Ask yourself: What was the best thing about today?

When you ask the question, you can think about the answer, and then you can say the answer in your mind.

Then, ask: *What do I look forward to tomorrow?*

This question makes you think about the future and what will happen that you are looking forward to.

Finally, ask: *What would you like to tell me next?*

Just let your mind relax into the nothing space, and you can even fall asleep. Your answer may come before you sleep or even in a dream, so take note of what you dreamed that night. Maybe even write it down.

Walking Meditation

This is one of my favourites, and I practise it nearly every day. It is a form of mindful meditation and a powerful way to focus, balance and take in your surroundings. You can do walking meditation by using this process:

1. Pick a path that you would like to walk on. It can be in a park, track or street in your neighbourhood.
2. You can wear your headphones if this helps you relax and listen to the music you enjoy. Note: If you are near traffic, it is wise to have the headphones on at a sound level so that you can hear outside noise.
3. While walking, take in your surroundings—the sky, trees, birds, houses. I often see the kangaroos staring me down when I walk past.
4. Use all your senses. How does your body feel? What does it feel like to be walking? How is the sound of your breath—laboured or not?

Mantra Meditation

This meditation is the repetition of a word, phrase or syllable. It helps bring your mind to the present as our voice helps us focus on the mantra. You can repeat this out loud by singing, humming, chanting, or do so silently. Lie or sit down; this can also be done standing up. Close your eyes if you feel like it, take three deep breaths, and then breathe normally.

Choose a mantra that resonates with you. There are many to choose from. If you are creating your own mantra, remember that you are making a statement, and choose something that aligns with your goals and aspirations.

Some are Hindu references to ancient Sanskrit, others are Buddhist mantras, and others are Hawaiian mantras.

Examples of Mantras That You Can Use. Pick One and Repeat it 108 Times:

'Om' or *'Aum'* means *it is, will be,* or *to become,* and it is a Sanskrit word that Hindus and Buddhists use. Often considered the sound of the universe and believed to have been present at the creation of the universe.

'I Love You; I'm Sorry; Please Forgive Me; Thank You' is from the Ho'oponopono prayer and translates to 'making things right' in ancient Hawaiian culture.

'I can and I will' is a famous English mantra. This mantra represents believing in yourself and your abilities and that you have the determination and willpower to do anything you want to do.

Visualisation

In this technique, I would also create a vision board to help view things prior to your meditation. Please see the 'Manifestation' chapter for a step-by-step guide on how to make a vision board.

1. Lie or sit down. Pick one thing that you would like to meditate on.
2. Imagine in detail what it would feel with your hands, taste with your mouth, smell with your nose, hear with your ears and see with your eyes. Use all your senses to describe what it is like to have what you want.
3. How would you feel if you had what you visualised? Joy, freedom, gratitude?
4. What can you do every day to reach your desired outcome?
5. Do you need to research and find out more information or study more to gain more knowledge in what you desire?
6. Each day, look at your vision board to remind yourself of all you have experienced when you imagine you have what you desire.

Loving-Kindness and Compassion Meditation

Some consider this a problematic form of meditation because it requires showing self-love and compassion to you and others. It is a mantra we can say while invoking feelings of love and kindness and really believing in what is being said. I have provided some examples below. Choose ones that resonate with you the most.

1. Lie or sit down; this can also be done standing up.
2. Close your eyes if you feel like it, take three deep breaths, and then breathe normally.
3. Focus on your heart chakra and notice your feelings and any sensations when saying this meditation.

Focus on Yourself and Say These Phrases:

1. May I be safe
2. May I be happy
3. May I be healthy
4. May my heart and mind awaken
5. May I be free from ill will, affliction and anxiety
6. May I love myself as I am

Focus on Others, Such as Someone You Love or a Dear Friend, and Say These Phrases:

1. May you be safe
2. May you be happy
3. May you be healthy
4. May your heart and mind awaken
5. May you be free from ill will, affliction and anxiety
6. May you love yourself as you are

Focus on Everyone and Say These Phrases:

1. May all be safe
2. May all be happy
3. May all be healthy
4. May everyone's hearts and minds awaken
5. May all be free from ill will, affliction and anxiety
6. May everyone love themselves as they are

Spiritual Meditation

Spiritual meditation is a practice in which we connect to our higher self, God, the creator, and the universe. It feels like a mystical experience as we go to the inner depths of who we are. Many forms of meditation can lead to spiritual meditation. Reaching this point in the experience can be a life-changing experience and an awakening of all the senses.

Some Forms of Meditation That Can Lead You to Experience a Spiritual State Are:

- Loving-Kindness and compassion meditation
- Guided connection with higher self-meditation
- Mantra meditation
- Mindful breathing

Mindful Breathing

This is a straightforward form of meditation as it focuses on breathwork to meditate.

1. Lie down, ready to go to sleep. Make yourself comfortable and close your eyes.
2. Inhale for ten counts. When you inhale, you fill up your diaphragm with air, expand your stomach area and bring the breath up to your throat. Again, please note that these

breathing exercises must be comfortable, so only do what feels right for you.

3. Hold for ten counts. Tense your body to keep the air in. Then, try to relax in this state.
4. Exhale for two counts. Expel the air through the mouth, releasing it first from the stomach area by squeezing your stomach muscles, then releasing your chest area and then all the air that is left in your diaphragm.
5. Repeat five times. While doing this breathwork, notice how you feel and relax any body part that feels tight or has tension.

If your mind wanders, then bring your thoughts back to your breath.

Awareness of the Body Meditation

This meditation technique involves focusing on your body from your feet to your head. It helps you relax, leading to a better night's sleep.

1. Lie down, ready to go to sleep. Make sure you are in a comfortable position and have removed all distractions.
2. Close your eyes, take three deep breaths, and then breathe normally.
3. Take note of your body; feel the weight on the bed.
4. Relax your face muscles. Think about how it feels.
5. Relax your neck and shoulders. Think about how they feel. Are they tight or sore?
6. Relax your back and stomach and think about how they feel. Are they sore? Are the muscles tight?
7. Relax your arms and hands next to your body. How do they feel?
8. Relax your hips, legs and feet and feel the tiredness and tension.
9. Feel all the physical sensations in your body and let them all release. If your focus starts to wander, slowly bring it back to where it had wandered.

10. You can then take three deep breaths and end the meditation by drifting off to sleep, or if you still have energy or tension that you want to release, you can repeat this from the feet to your head.

Guided Meditation

Guided meditation is an excellent approach to getting started in meditation. During guided meditation, you follow the instructions, which can help you relax. You do not have to think about what you must do; follow what is said.

Pick a guided meditation that resonates with you now.

1. Lie down, ready to go to sleep, making sure you are in a comfortable position and have removed all distractions.
2. Start the recorded meditation. If you are listening on a mobile phone, make sure the light is dim, and you have activated the do-not-disturb function on your phone.
3. Close your eyes and follow the instructions given in the guided meditation.

Meditation is a powerful tool that can help us find balance, clarity and peace in our everyday lives. It isn't about sitting in silence; it's about taking a moment to breathe, reflect and connect with our inner selves. Remember, there's no right or wrong way to meditate. It's all about what feels right for you. Start small, be patient with yourself, and gradually build your practise. As you continue, you'll likely notice a positive shift in your mindset, reduced stress and a greater sense of well-being.

Beyond these benefits, meditation can also be a vital tool for self-actualisation. Regularly turning inward and quieting the mind, you can gain deeper insights into your true self, uncover your passions and align more closely with your life's purpose. Embrace meditation as a daily practice, and let it guide you on your journey to becoming the best version of yourself. Happy meditating!

MANIFESTATION

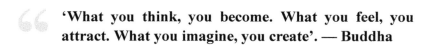

> 'What you think, you become. What you feel, you attract. What you imagine, you create'. — Buddha

Have you ever imagined how much fun it would be to have a genie to grant your every wish? What if I was to tell you this power lies within you, without a lamp to rub in sight!

Manifestation is like having your own genie; it's all about focusing on your desires and working towards making them a reality. Based on the Law of Attraction and the Power of Positive Thinking, your thoughts and intentions can create your reality.

The three laws of attraction follow the steps of attracting, creating and allowing, which work in tandem with the power of positive thinking. When we maintain a positive mindset, we attract more positive energy. This propels us towards our best life.

We can visualise ourselves as a magnet. Positive thoughts are like tiny metal shavings drawn towards us, empowering us to create our desired reality.

On the other hand, negative thoughts are also attracted to us but act as heavy metal weights. They block us in and keep us from harnessing positive energy. Negative thinking acts as a barrier, impeding our growth.

By focusing on positive thinking and maintaining a clear vision of our goals, we can harness the power of manifestation. Just like in the tale of the genie, the magic lies within us, waiting to be realised. Ask, and you shall receive! The origins of manifestation practices can be traced back to various spiritual and philosophical traditions. Ancient teachings often emphasise the power of the mind and the importance of aligning one's thoughts with one's intentions.

Manifestation is based on the belief that the universe is abundant and ready to provide what we need if we ask with intention and clarity. It's like sending out a signal that aligns with the energy of the universe, drawing our desires toward us. Another foundational aspect of manifestation is subconscious anchoring. Subconscious anchoring is the process of repetition through meditation, writing, chanting and repeatedly focusing on our goals and desires, which embeds these thoughts in our subconscious mind. When these thoughts are deeply ingrained, our subconscious gets on board, becoming the steering captain of the ship in ways that align with our higher good.

MANIFESTATION METHODS

Meditation

As mentioned in the earlier chapter on 'Meditation', many different meditations can help us attract what we desire. A guided meditation for manifestation can help us focus on what we want. Remember to try to repeat this regularly and start with a short meditation first to help get into the rhythm.

Positive Subliminal Messages and Affirmations

Positive subliminal messages and affirmations are compelling tools for manifestation. As mentioned in our earlier chapters 'Meditation' and 'Cleansing Your Space', subliminal messages are layered underneath music and sound you can listen to. We repeat affirmations out loud or in our minds. As mentioned in earlier chapters, they work by repro-gramming our subconscious thoughts, the beliefs and attitudes that shape our reality. By listening to positive subliminal messages and using positive affirmations, we can align our subconscious mind with our desires, making it easier to attract and create what we want. There are a variety of subliminal audios, with anything from attracting money and miracles to manifesting and even helping us quit a habit. When we listen to these consecutively, for about twenty-one days, they can reprogram our subconscious thoughts.

Gratitude

The chapter 'Gratitude' shows us that this is the superpower of self-actualisation and a powerhouse for manifesting—supercharged! Showing gratitude for what we appreciate and want to manifest brings us a step closer to what we want. Practising gratitude is like sparking a cycle of positive energy; it acts as a catalyst that enhances and acceler-ates the manifestation process, ensuring your desires align with the universe's abundant offerings.

Release Negativity

Releasing negativity is a crucial step in the manifestation process. It's something that many do not realise can hold us back from that beau-tiful cycle. We must associate positive energy with our experiences and release negativity. This involves acknowledging and accepting nega-tive thoughts and emotions and consciously letting them go. The patterns and experiences we face that no longer serve us are the lessons we are here to learn in this life. Remember, each pattern is a choice or decision. Acknowledge the pattern, honour the experience, and then release it. If we react the same way we usually do, it means that we have not learned the necessary lesson. We delve into this more in Part Three.

When we picture our life purpose as a beautiful boat on a voyage, negativity is like sharp rocks shredding the rudder, preventing us from moving with the wind filling our sails provided by the universe to sweep us effortlessly to our goals!

Creating a Vision Board

A vision board is one of my favourite practices for manifestation.

We can often think about the future and what we want it to be like, so we can make a vision board that reflects this. Creating a vision board may seem silly, but adding pictures of what we love and what we want can help us find our purpose and manifest what we want. Add statements and words that mean something to us. This is our board. Our vision for our life. Do not worry about what others think or say about our board because they can create their own board! When we look at the completed board, it will show a story, and this is our story. Focusing regularly on the board can reinforce what we want, and then our purpose can be formed.

I completed my first vision board in December 2023. A few months later, I could see that everything on that board was lining up to fruition in 2024. Had I tapped into a superpower by manifesting what I wanted? Normally, I thought I should have completed some kind of visual board on New Year's Eve, but I never acted on the thought. I would always set my New Year's resolution or sometimes even write down what I wanted. Still, I must say that searching and printing out photos to put them on a board was something new to me.

I would recommend creating a vision board for everyone. This is something anybody of any age can do. Also, if we change our mind about what we want during the year, we can take down the photo that reminds us of the old and replace it with a new desire.

How to Create a Vision Board

1. Think about your goals.
2. Begin by creating a quiet space for yourself. Reflect on why you're making the vision board. Is it a goal board for specific achievements, a reflection board for introspection or a themed board to help you find your purpose?
3. Consider what you want to manifest or achieve. Is it related to money, health, travel, romance or study, or is it a general board encompassing various aspects of your life?
4. It is essential to be honest with yourself about what you truly want. If your goals seem huge, break them into smaller, manageable parts. Think about what is achievable within the time set for this board.
5. Envision items that are attainable in your life. Avoid filling the board with unrealistic items, which might have the opposite effect. However, don't hesitate to include a few of your biggest dreams and aspirations as you put these desires into the universe.
6. Choose the type of board you'll use—corkboard, poster board or another type. Gather your project's necessary materials, such as pins, tape or glue.
7. Collect images from personal photos or online sources. Consider using: newspaper clippings, quotes from books, affirmations, old cards, receipts, souvenirs.
8. Choose your photos and quotes. Start creating the scene you want on your vision board. Select items that align with your goals and vision and what you want to manifest in your life. Take your time with this step.
9. Place them on the board. Begin arranging the photos, quotes and other items on your board. Make sure everything is visible. If you have too many items, you might need to cull some. The items that remain should represent what you aim for in life. By thoughtfully crafting your vision board, you create a visual representation of your goals and aspirations,

helping you stay focused and motivated on your journey to manifesting your dreams.

10. Start pinning and taping the items on the board.
11. When you have finished, stand back and look at the board. It should bring you joy, excitement and inspiration and put a smile on your face. Take the time to regularly look at your vision board to keep you on track.

Crystals

When we are in the crystal store, set the intention of what we want the crystal to do, and then we will be attracted to the most potent stones. They will amplify the energy surrounding what we want. We may also prefer to wear crystals as jewellery. These can be any form, such as a necklace, bracelet, etc. When we trust ourselves, our intuition will pick the best crystals for us. Below are some of the most popular stones for manifesting.

- Rose Quartz: the love crystal, attracts love and self-love
- Carnelian: attracts prosperity, boosts self-esteem, awakens creativity, and brings good luck and confidence
- Moonstone: considered to be the love stone. It is calming and great for balancing emotions and inspiring new beginnings.
- Pyrite: Fools gold: abundance, prosperity, and luck are the properties of this perfect stone.
- Tigers Eye: great manifestation stone attracting abundance and leading you towards the life of your dreams. It is empowering and protective. Aids in mental clarity and inspiration.
- Clear Quartz: a master healer, amplifying your energy and connecting to your vibration

Dream Incubation

Dream incubation is a method of asking a question before going to bed and receiving an answer in a dream. The answer can come directly or metaphorically, requiring you to interpret the story presented. If the dream feels rushed, try to slow it down, observe and consider the energy surrounding it.

For example, suppose we want to change careers. We might dream directly of the desired job, working at the company we want. This is a clear answer. However, if we dream of a different job that brings us joy and contentment, this can be a positive sign, too. It suggests we're on the right path to manifesting a new reality, even if the job isn't exactly what we initially envisioned. See the chapter on 'Dreams' for more in-depth insights.

The 369 Rule

The 369 rule is a straightforward rule. We write down what we want to manifest three times in the morning, six times during the middle of the day, and nine times at the end of the day. It reinforces our intention so we can bring into reality what we desire. There is a variation to this rule: the 333 rule, in which we create an affirmation around what we want to manifest and write it down thirty-three times for three days.

Act as If It Has Already Happened

Acting as if your manifestation has already occurred can be a powerful tool. For example, if you want to manifest money, act as though it has already arrived. You might start by adding a little extra cash to your wallet. Make important decisions without stressing about money. I'm not suggesting you spend money you don't have, but rather, if you need to make a purchase and have the funds, approach it without negative energy. When meditating, visualise yourself in the situation you desire as though it is happening in the present moment. Speak positively about it. For example, I could have said, *'I'm trying to write a book. I'm not sure if I can'*, but instead, I said, *'I'm writing a book. I am going to help someone'*.

By acting as if your desired reality has already come to pass, you align your mindset with abundance. This positive approach helps bring that reality into your physical world, reinforcing the manifestation process.

Manifestation Jar

I highly recommend this method as you entrust your dreams and goals to the universe to take care of them. Just complete it and leave it alone.

1. Choose a jar that you like and will want to use. One with a lid is best; the size will depend on how many things you want to add.
2. Write down your wishes on small pieces of paper. Use a different piece for each wish you want to manifest and fold them in half. If it is money, put some notes in the jar. Add photos or images and even crystals or small items that symbolise what you want.
3. When adding all the items and notes to the jar, invoke feelings of happiness and excitement or perhaps joy.
4. Once the jar is full, you must remove your attachment to the outcome. Release the results to the universe.
5. Now you leave it! Let the universe take care of the results, so all you need to do is wait and keep yourself in a positive mood and vibration. Do not be impatient and add more things to the jar, as this may break the manifestation cycle of the wishes that you already had in the jar. Act in faith that the universe has your back.

Manifesting can bring what we desire out of nowhere, but most of the time, we still must work at it. For instance, I manifested that writing this book would be a success, but I still had to choose the chapters, write the book, edit, publish and sell the book.

There are processes and actions I must take to get me to the desired outcome: a successful book that will help others. This is why it is essential to note our small steps to get the result. Appreciating those small steps helps the manifestation process. I am enjoying writing this book; yes, sometimes I must think hard about what I want to write, but I am still positive about the process. I might need to take a break from what I am doing as I need to think about the chapters and enjoy my life outside the book's writing, but I am still in a state of appreciation.

The more we see things with positivity, the more we enjoy the moment, the more we change. Our moods and thoughts change for the positive; it is all relative. Joy brings us fulfilment. Material things are not going to bring fulfilment. We may have saved up our whole life to buy a car that we really want. Once we have it, we are happy, but then we ask, *'What is next?'* A car can bring us joy, but the pleasure is even greater if we are grateful every time we drive our dream car. Suppose we appreciate the car that brings us happiness daily and decide to save for a better model. In that case, we should remain thankful for the current car until the day we get another one. This is because the first car manifested our earlier dreams and wishes. The joy surrounding the car should not diminish now that we have it; otherwise, we are not honouring the value of our manifestations. We must remember that manifestation is our dreams, wishes and hopes that come into realisation. Once we have that, we shouldn't devalue it because we want something better.

UNDERSTANDING DELAYS IN MANIFESTATION

Sometimes, our manifestations can be delayed if the timing isn't right, especially if what we manifest is connected to our soul contract. In 'Remembering Who We Are', we explore the concept of soul contracts. What we want will happen in divine time. In other words, the universe will make it happen at precisely the right time, even at the last moment.

Another reason for manifestation delays is that we may still need to learn specific lessons related to our desires. For instance, it becomes difficult for our manifestation to materialise if we focus on manifesting money but have negative beliefs about it—thinking we will never have enough or wanting it too desperately. We must remove our attachment to money and overcome the scarcity mindset to receive more.

This principle applies to all aspects of life, not just money. In 'Leave Your Ego at the Door', we discuss ego and attachment. When we let go of these attachments, we allow our manifestations to come to fruition. By releasing our grip on what we desire, we create space for abundance to flow into our lives.

How Do You Know if Your Manifestation Is in Progress?

Now, we may start having dreams or visions of what we desire. So, as mentioned earlier, with dream incubation, the aspects or the symbolism of what we manifest may appear in our dreams.

Conversations with Others

Sometimes, others will mention the exact things we are trying to manifest without knowing our intentions. When someone brings up our desires out of the blue, it's a sign that our manifestation is drawing near. This indicates that what we have been doing is working, and our manifestation is taking shape.

Déjà Vu

Déjà vu occurs when we experience something and feel like it has happened before. We might be talking to a friend and suddenly think we've already experienced this. Or perhaps it's more of a vague feeling of familiarity. Experiencing déjà vu about our manifestation means we are pulling this reality from another dimension into our current experience, indicating that it is becoming a reality.

Seeing the Puzzle Pieces Come Together

When we notice parts of the puzzle joining together, it's a sign that our manifestation is coming soon. If our desire is significant, getting to where we want to be may require several pieces to fall into place first. When we see these elements aligning, it's a sign that our manifestation is on its way. Keep an eye out for these signs and remain positive—the desired outcome is taking shape.

Trust the Process

Manifestation requires us to trust the process. When we genuinely feel happy about what we desire without being attached to the outcome, it's a sign that the manifestation is close to becoming our reality. Sometimes, this trust leads to significant changes in our lives—things may shift, alter, or fall away. Friendships, relationships or jobs may end, making space for new opportunities, manifestations and growth. This happens because those aspects of our lives no longer align with who we are and what we want.

Trust that these changes are for the better. By leaving it in the hands of the universe, we allow our desires to manifest in the best possible way. Rest assured, it will all work out for the better.

NUMBERS

 'Numbers are the universal language offered by the deity to humans as confirmation of the truth'. — St. Augustine of Hippo

Numbers have played an intriguing part in human history, not just for counting! Humans have held a fascination for patterns and repetition for aeons. I wonder, if I had known more when I started my book-keeping business, what might I have gleaned?

You might remember the Pythagorean Theorem from high school maths. It's the basis of geometry and maths. The ancient Greek mathematician and philosopher Pythagoras created this theorem and is also credited with creating modern numerology. He and his students studied and embraced the spiritual significance of numbers. The ancient Greeks, Egyptians and Babylonians found numbers' mystical meaning fascinating.

In the Bible, some numbers are repeated. This indicates their importance and a spiritual message. For example, the number forty appears repeatedly, associated with trials, purification or preparation. There are the forty days of the Flood, Moses's forty days on Mount Sinai and Jesus's forty days in the desert.

Ancient Egyptians believed in the power of repetition in their spiritual practices. The repetition of specific images or hieroglyphs in tombs and sacred texts was intended to reinforce their protective qualities.

Gematria, a Jewish Kabbalah practice, involves calculating the numerical value of Hebrew words, names and phrases for spiritual insight.

Have you heard of the Golden Ratio? This magic number is hiding in plain sight, influencing everything from the spirals of seashells to the proportions of the world's most famous artworks. What makes this number so unique? Symbolised as Phi (Φ), with a value of approximately 1.618, The Golden Ratio has been associated with the Parthenon in Greece to Leonardo da Vinci's famous '*Vitruvian Man*'. The number of petals on a flower, pine cones, galaxies, sequences in music and even hurricanes follow this ratio in their patterns and growth.

We contain evidence of the Golden Ratio, too.

Look at your fingers, and you'll notice each one is divided into three sections by your knuckles. Measure the length of one section (from the tip of your finger to the first knuckle), then measure the entire length of your finger. Now, divide the total length by the length of one section. You guessed it! The Golden Ratio. This makes us wonder about our universe's grand design, doesn't it?

We may start to see repetitive numbers and patterns. When we pay attention to what is happening around us, we can start to understand the messages these numbers convey.

I frequently notice these numbers on my mobile phone. I may pick up my phone at 11:11, or a message came in at that exact time. I pause to reflect on what I have been thinking about or my actions. It is up to me to stop and note what is being shown. You may wake up at a certain time and see the numbers on your digital clock or phone. Some people see them as number plates or an amount on a receipt. Again, I smile; as a bookkeeper and a BAS Agent, I know what mysteries may have been sitting before me or even in the tape when measuring fabric!

You will notice the majesty of your surroundings, helping to shift your consciousness.

HERE ARE SOME OF MINE I HAVE NOTED:

111 - Something new is about to start, or a new opportunity will present itself. I need to pay attention to avoid missing it.

1111 - Trust my intuition and believe I am on the right path.

222 – Restore balance, harmony and trust in my personal and business relationships.

1221—Keep positivity, strength and motivation at the centre, embrace change and keep an open mind.

So, what is the lesson we are being shown? When we actively pay attention to our surroundings and the hints beneath the surface, we find ourselves in a self-empowered space. There can be a blossoming feeling of intrigue and joy—there is more to life than we once thought! Sometimes, we can experience turmoil during the process of awakening, which we discuss in this book, but the reward is beyond words. We start a magnificent quest that is anything but boring. Numbers and patterns are yet another indicator that we are all connected. When we feel that connection, the universe, our higher power and our soul all harmonise.

ARE WE WHAT WE EAT?

 'Let food be thy medicine and medicine be thy food'.
— Hippocrates

Have you ever contemplated that the food on your plate might be nudging you toward self-actualisation? Let's munch on this deliciously intriguing idea.

We are so bombarded with food options in our world. Food is our life-line, providing essential nutrients that support our health and well-being. Our culture and religion often influence our dietary choices. Vibrational foods, considered spiritual, can support you on your self-actualisation journey. I am Italian, so cooking and sharing food is culturally significant in my family. Food in Italy is not just about suste-nance; it's about community, family and celebration. Meals are often a time for gathering loved ones, sharing stories and celebrating life's moments, both big and small. In my family, the emphasis on fresh, high-quality ingredients and the love for regional specialities creates a passion for food, an appreciation for the pleasures of life and the importance of savouring each moment.

In Hindu cultures, especially in Ashrams, there is a strong belief in growing organic food nurtured and prepared with great care. This practice imbues the food with good energy, which we absorb, helping to raise our vibration. Fresh foods that have not been interfered with contain prana, or life force, contributing to our physical and spiritual well-being. Consuming these high-prana foods can significantly enhance our spiritual journey. We cannot underestimate how foods can impact not only our physical health and well-being but also our spiritual health. We are indeed what we eat.

ALLERGIES AND PERSONAL EXPERIENCES

Allergies can cause severe reactions to certain foods. Common allergies include sesame, nuts, eggs, shellfish, soybeans, wheat and milk, causing symptoms like itchy eyes, rashes, vomiting and diarrhoea. More severe reactions, such as anaphylaxis, can be life-threatening and require immediate treatment with epinephrine (Mayo Clinic Staff, 2024). My daughter, for example, is allergic to sesame seeds, so we avoid them entirely when she is around.

Personal experiences with food can profoundly impact our choices. My mother once got salmonella poisoning from meat, leading her to hospitalisation. Not long after, my uncle suffered from severe food poisoning. These experiences influenced my family's dietary habits, resulting in the purchase of high-quality fresh meats and produce. I observed my healthy and active 91-year-old father and noted his predominantly plant-based diet. He consumes lentil soup, pasta, bread with ricotta cheese, various bean soups, fruits and occasional fish. This diet seems to contribute to his longevity and health.

HIGH- VS. LOW-VIBRATIONAL FOODS

Low-vibrational foods include processed foods, items with long shelf lives, food colourings, additives, preservatives and alcohol. Overripe, stale or spoiled fruits and vegetables lose much of their pranic energy.

They can contribute to a dull, heavy feeling in the body. Eating high-vibrational foods means choosing fresh, colourful and nutrient-rich options that fuel our bodies efficiently. How we eat affects our physical health and influences how we think, feel and experience life. In the 'Chakras' chapter, we discuss which high-vibrational foods are aligned to which chakra.

MINDFUL EATING AND PRANA

Mindful eating, which means being present and fully experiencing our meals, can transform our relationship with food. When we practise mindful eating, we often report better digestion, increased energy and more enjoyment. This practice makes making healthy choices and managing weight easier without resorting to fad diets. Mindful eating leads to a healthier relationship with our food, ourselves and the world, as they are all interconnected.

HERE ARE SOME PRACTICAL STEPS FOR MINDFUL EATING:

- **Set your intention**: Decide to practise mindful eating to honour your body and nourish it properly.
- **Be grateful**: Take a moment to say grace or express thanks for the food you are about to eat, acknowledging all the effort to get it to your table.
- **Eat fresh and local**: Whenever possible, choose locally sourced and seasonal foods, which are often fresher and more nutrient-rich.
- **Balance your meals**: Ensure your diet is balanced and nutritious, incorporating various foods that provide essential vitamins and minerals.

NUTRITIONAL NEEDS

Incorporating diversity in our diet and ensuring that our food contains vitamins and minerals is essential for a healthy lifestyle. Vitamins and minerals are vital for our metabolism, bones, blood cells, growth and nervous system. Protein is crucial for muscle repair, tissue health and energy. Amino acids from protein produce enzymes and hormones. A lack of protein can lead to fatigue, weakness, a slow metabolism and anaemia. Micronutrient deficiencies can cause visible and dangerous health conditions. Still, they can also lead to less clinically notable reductions in energy level, mental clarity and overall capacity. (World Health Organisation, 2024).

RESEARCH ON MINDFULNESS AND FOOD

A review by Michopoulou et al. (2020) found that mindfulness helped people with food disorders. They observed Buddhist monks, who ate 15–19g of protein and meditated three to four times a day, maintained stable health compared to regular people who consumed 30g of protein daily.

What we eat is a topic filled with emotion and significance, impacting celebrations, gatherings and everyday meals. We each have our reasons, beliefs and traditions that shape our dietary choices. If we maintain health, there is no one right way to eat. It's about making the best decisions for us.

By consciously choosing foods that support our physical and spiritual health, we pave the way for deeper self-actualisation, aligning our daily habits with our highest aspirations. Choosing high-vibrational foods enhances our physical well-being and uplifts our spirit, helping us connect more deeply with our true selves.

Note: Whenever making significant changes to your diet, always seek advice from a nutritional expert or your general practitioner to ensure it's safe and appropriate for your individual health needs.

WATER H2O

 'In one drop of water are found all the secrets of all the oceans'. — Kahlil Gibran

Water, a lifeline to the human body, is crucial for survival, but did you know it holds energy and memory? Water is vital to our existence. It is in the sea, the atmosphere, lakes, underground and inside our bodies. It envelops us when rain falls from the sky, cleansing the air and giving it a fresh rain smell known as petrichor. Water is a resource we often take for granted. If you live in a country with clean drinking water, consider yourself blessed.

BODY WATER

Approximately 60 per cent of our bodies consist of water. Drinking plenty of water daily isn't just a good idea for our health; it's critical to feeling our best. Water is vital for hydration and waste removal. It regulates temperature, lubricates joints and protects tissues. It aids digestion, maintains blood pressure and supports kidney and skin health. Water boosts physical and mental performance to peak levels.

DRINKING WATER

Staying hydrated is key to good health. But not all water is equal in quality. Mohd Nani et al. (2016) found that deep-sea water, with its high magnesium content, can benefit health. Desalination can help us regain the beneficial minerals in deep-sea water. These minerals delay fat cell production and offer other health benefits.

It's essential to be mindful of the water quality we drink. Water treated with reverse osmosis or chlorination is low in nutrients and not as beneficial. Instead, opt for water that retains natural minerals to maintain good health.

WATER AND OUR INTENTIONS

This is where water studies get very exciting! Radin et al. (2006) investigated whether our intentions could affect water properties. In their study, approximately 2,000 people in Tokyo prayed aloud with gratitude towards water in a laboratory 5,000 miles away. The group was shown images of the location of the water and two bottles that were inside a shielded chamber with the words PRAYER FOR WATER overlaid on the bottled water. They were not shown the other two bottles that were placed in a box in a quiet location on another floor in a building that housed a shielded room. After thirty-six hours, small amounts of water were placed in Petri dishes and put in the freezer for a minimum of three hours at -25°C to -30°C and then photographed. The most beautiful, symmetric crystals formed in the water exposed to the prayer. The conclusion was that intention may influence water structure, as the ones with the prayer of gratitude were the most pleasing shapes.

If positive intentions can affect water's structure, I wonder what negative thoughts can do.

WATER AND NEGATIVE AIR IONS IMPROVING OUR AIR QUALITY

Water and negative air ions (NAIs) have been shown to improve air quality. Juang et al. (2018) noted that significant NAIs are found near waterfalls and seashores. Known as the 'waterfall effect', these negative ions are released when water collides with itself, such as in waterfalls or the ocean. These ions, known for over 100 years, are widely used for air cleaning. No wonder we feel refreshed and rejuvenated near waterfalls or the sea.

Borra et al. (1996) investigated electrical and chemical changes in forests during mist and thunderstorms. They found that higher levels of gaseous ions from point discharges were closely linked to thunderstorms, which helped clear pollutants from the air. Mist and fog also produced NAIs.

The synergistic relationship between the Earth and the atmosphere reminds us of our connection to the natural world. It highlights the intricate balance of our Earth's ecosystem.

DEEP-SEA WATER

Since I was little, I remember always being told that the beach was the place to reinvigorate us and resolve issues we may have been having with our skin and nearly everything else. Going for a swim or just being in the sea would solve the problem. Mohd Nani et al. (2016) reviewed the benefits of deep-sea water. They found that deep-sea water, water over 200m deep, contains more minerals compared to shallow-sea water. Minerals such as magnesium, calcium, potassium, sodium and chondrite are abundant in deep-sea water. These minerals offer health benefits for high cholesterol, cardiovascular disease, obesity, diabetes and asthma. They also reduce fatigue and repair muscle damage from exercise.

BLUE SPACES

Walking into the water at the beach and enjoying the texture, smell, warmth or coolness of the water, even on a hot day, can be incredibly re-energising. We can practise our mindfulness while doing so. White et al. (2020) studied blue space's effect on health and well-being. It found benefits like lower temperatures and increased activity. It reduced stress and provided participants with more time with friends and family. Being near rivers, lakes or the ocean offers many benefits.

No doubt, water is a magical elixir. It's essential for life and has fascinating properties. Water is extraordinary. It improves air quality and affects our emotions. It also plays a role in our bodies. Knowing its importance can boost our health and well-being. It can also connect us to nature.

NATURE, THE GREAT HEALER

 'Look deep into nature, and then you will understand everything better'. — Albert Einstein

Nature provides us with an abundance of wonders and resources. It's no surprise that this world was designed for the human experience and all living beings. We have everything we need to thrive in nature, from the air we breathe to the food and water that sustain us. The natural world offers endless chances for growth and healing. It reminds us of the harmony between life and the environment.

GROUNDING

Grounding is the practice of connecting with the Earth. Grounding profoundly affects our body, mind and spirit. This connection helps us feel centred and gives us the time and space to evaluate our lives. Let's explore some ways to ground ourselves. We'll also look at research on the benefits of connecting with nature.

One simple way to ground yourself is by standing on grass without shoes. Have you ever tried it? The sensation of the cool grass under your feet can be incredibly calming. Walking in nature or going to the beach are great ways to connect with the Earth. Grounding aligns our bodies with nature. It restores our well-being if we feel off-balance.

I remember feeling particularly stressed one day and decided to walk in a nearby park. As I walked on the grass and listened to the birds, my tension melted away. Not only am I exercising self-care by doing this, but it gives me the feeling of being refreshed.

THE BENEFITS OF NATURE

Did you know that an undeveloped natural area in a city benefits nearby residents? Greenspaces provide a breath of fresh air, literally and figuratively. Isn't it amazing how even the trees lined along a street can improve our well-being?

Research proves that nature exposure yields measurable health improvements. For instance, Twohig-Bennett et al. (2018) found that greenspaces reduced diabetes, heart disease and deaths from all causes. Another study by White et al. (2020) highlighted the sound-mitigating effects of greenspaces. These findings reassure us that something as simple as being in nature can profoundly affect our health.

Walking in nature offers more benefits than walking on a treadmill. Twohig-Bennett et al. (2018) also found that walking in nature improved mental health, with effects lasting up to three months. In the 'Meditation' chapter, I explain how to meditate while walking. This can enhance the benefits even more.

FOREST BATHING

Forest bathing, or 'Shinrin-yoku', is another fantastic way to connect with nature. Introduced by the Japanese government in 1982, this practice involves visiting a forest for relaxation. It aims to breathe in the volatile substances, called phytoncides, released by trees (Li et al., 2007). This practice is about physical health and spiritual and emotional well-being. Isn't it fascinating how something as simple as walking in a forest can rejuvenate us? The forest stimulates our senses. The smell of cedar alone lowers blood pressure.

Li et al. (2007) also found that forest bathing increased white blood cells. It boosted the number and activity of natural killer (NK) cells that fight infections. The benefits of a three-day, two-night forest bathing trip lasted for more than thirty days. This suggests that regular time in nature is key to these health benefits. Monthly forest bathing could keep people's NK cell levels high. Li (2010) suggested that forest bathing trips might prevent cancer. Isn't that remarkable?

TREE-HUGGING

Tree-hugging might seem a quirky pastime for nature lovers, but research shows physical and mental health benefits. Spending time with our timber friends can significantly reduce stress levels. For instance, a study by Park et al. (2010) found that those who walked in a forest had lower cortisol levels than those who walked in a city. Cortisol is the stress hormone. So lower levels mean nature helps us relax. Also, nature can lower blood pressure and heart rate. This helps heart health. Nature's calming effect might explain why we feel at peace in a forest.

Trees can also boost your immune system. As stated earlier, they emit phytoncides, organic compounds with antimicrobial properties. Li (2010) found that inhaling these compounds boosts NK cells, which are vital for fighting infections and tumours. Next time you're in the woods, take deep breaths of fresh air; it will do wonders for your immune system.

Spending time with trees can uplift your mood and improve your mental health. Broader research shows that nature exposure boosts mood and reduces anxiety. For instance, a review by Bratman et al. (2015) highlighted the mental health benefits of being in nature, including improved affect and cognition. Activities like tree-hugging and spending time with trees can be a form of mindfulness. This connection can reduce feelings of loneliness and isolation, which are common contributors to depression and anxiety.

Isn't it fascinating how hugging a tree can provide a unique sensory experience? The texture of the bark, the solidity of the trunk and the natural energy of the tree can be soothing and grounding. This tactile stimulation can calm, like other touch therapies. Also, nature increases alpha wave activity in the brain, which links to a relaxed, awake state. Research by Ulrich et al. (1991) and more recent studies state that being in nature promotes relaxation and mental clarity.

ECOTHERAPY

Nature-based interventions, or ecotherapy, can significantly boost mental health. A meta-analysis by Marseille et al. (2019) found that nature-based therapies can reduce depression and anxiety. Engaging with nature helps us reconnect with our world. It fosters peace and well-being. A walk in the forest, sitting by a stream or hugging a tree reminds us of our connection to nature.

Outdoor activities like walking barefoot on grass, forest bathing and hugging trees are great ways to connect with nature. Benefits include reducing stress, improving immune function and enhancing overall mood and mental health. So, the next time you find yourself near a tree or a patch of grass, take a moment to ground yourself. If you have read 'Water H_2O', you will now understand that a walking meditation, sitting under a tree and a dip in the ocean supplies us with an amazing environment for self-actualisation!

Note: It is important to note that these activities may not be suitable for everyone. If you have health concerns or doubts, consult a doctor.

DREAMS

 'Who looks outside, dreams; who looks inside, awakes'. — Carl Jung

Our dreams can be emotional experiences, sensory adventures or filled with ideas and images. This is our unconscious mind being active. Waking up and remembering what the dream was about can be a challenge, or it might make us wake up startled, and we can recall every detail with frightening accuracy.

Dreams stem from our subconscious mind. They reflect our experiences, beliefs, desires, fears and the expectations of others. The subconscious mind is powerful. It holds our intuition, beliefs and feelings. It works even while we sleep. The conscious brain, however, shuts down during sleep.

When you dream about what you are manifesting, this is yet another sign that your new reality is incoming! As noted in the 'Manifestations' chapter, asking for what we want before sleep can help.

Studies show that we dream during Rapid Eye Movement (REM) sleep cycles. We are more likely to remember our dreams during this stage.

A study by Christina Marzano and her colleagues, published in the *Journal of Neuroscience*, found that theta and alpha brain waves in sleep predict dream recall. I find this fascinating. However, studying dreams is a challenge for researchers. They must awaken subjects, either spontaneously or by provoking them, to analyse their dreams.

The study involved sixty-five participants. They slept for two nights at a research centre. The first night was undisturbed to establish a baseline sleep pattern. On the second night, participants were awakened in the last five minutes of Stage 2 of sleep. The study identified five stages of REM sleep: Delta, Theta, Alpha, Sigma and Beta. Higher frontal theta activity during REM sleep correlated with better dream recall.

Nielsen et al. (2015) examined how food affects dreams in a study called 'Food and dreams: Multicultural Perceptions'. They found a link between vivid dreams and dream recall. It examined eating organic foods and brief fasting versus unhealthy food.

Waking up during the REM stage can help us remember our dreams. Foods that affect our energy and fullness during the day can also impact our sleep and dreams at night. Nielsen et al. (2015) found that dairy products sparked offbeat and unsettling dreams in many people's experiences. Late-night eating can cause gas, bloating, cramps and diarrhoea. These symptoms can affect our sleep and dreams.

DREAMS AND SPIRITUALITY

A spiritual view of dreams can connect the mind and soul in new ways. Have you ever woken up feeling like you received a message from beyond? While we sleep, our subconscious minds can open to receive messages from our loved ones who have passed away, angels, spirit guides and our higher selves. These messages can offer support, advice and warnings about our lives. It's comforting to know that we are never truly alone and that help is available, even when we are not awake.

Dreams are fascinating because they allow us to explore different realities. In dreams, we might see other dimensions or timelines. We may even glimpse past lives. These experiences can offer valuable insights into our identity and why we are here. By studying these alternate realities, we can better understand ourselves and our place in the universe.

Did you know our dreams can teach us how to use our innate gifts and skills? Many of us have special abilities related to energy healing, intuition and psychic talents. Still, we might not know how to tap into them. Our dreams can show us how to use our abilities. We can then grow and help others. It's like having a personal tutor guiding us through the mysteries of our own potential.

Symbols play a crucial role in our dreams. These symbolic messages help us understand what steps we need to take to move forward in our lives. By heeding these symbols, we can unlock deeper personal growth and healing.

VIVID AND LUCID DREAMS

There is a difference between a vivid dream and a lucid one. A vivid dream can be very memorable but not necessarily lucid. A lucid dream feels more real and lifelike, and we can even control the narrative. Sometimes, messages are sent through these vivid or lucid dreams.

Vivid Dreams: We remember the dream upon waking. But we do not know we are dreaming while it happens. Vivid dreams are the gateway to our unconscious mind. These dreams feel real and immersive, yet we cannot control them. REM sleep is when they typically take place. We may recall vivid images of our past lives, but it might be challenging to recognise them as such.

Lucid Dreams: In a lucid dream, we are asleep but aware that we are dreaming. It feels like we are there and might even be able to control the dream's events. Lucid dreaming usually happens in REM sleep and can be a very emotional experience. We might suffer from sleep paralysis during this time. According to Saunders et al. (2016), 55 per cent of people have experienced at least one lucid dream in their lifetime, and 23 per cent experience it once a month or more.

Recording our dreams can help us recall and analyse them. When we wake up, capturing the dream details in notes or voice recordings can preserve the memory. It's beneficial to note who was in the dream, how you felt, where you were, what you were doing, any images or symbols, themes, feelings, messages and any lessons learned. This is a fascinating process, as you can read or listen much later and reflect on what was going on in your life at the time. Keeping your personal record of dreams helps you to decipher what your subconscious may be trying to tell you.

PRACTICAL TIPS FOR BETTER SLEEP AND DREAM RECALL

Leonardo da Vinci said, '*Why does the eye see a thing more clearly in dreams than the imagination when awake?*' Dreams can help us solve problems. They let our imagination run wild, leading to new ideas.

For better sleep and dream recall:

- Try to go to bed and wake up at the same time each day.
- Ensure your pillow and mattress are comfortable.
- Maintain the ideal sleep temperature, around 18.3 degrees Celsius (65 degrees Fahrenheit).
- Avoid screens one to two hours before bed to help your mind relax.
- Keep your room dark; consider replacing window furnishings if necessary.
- Limit caffeine and alcohol intake before bedtime.

DREAM INTERPRETATIONS

The first recorded dream interpretation is from 2700 BC, written by a Sumerian priest-king, Gudea, who ruled Lagash. This Babylonian work is held in the Penn Museum in Philadelphia. In the 1900s, psychologist

Sigmund Freud wrote *The Interpretation of Dreams*. It laid the foundation for modern dream interpretation. Carl Jung's *Memories, Dreams, Reflection*s also discussed the significance of dreams. However, he diverged from Freud, who emphasised that all dreams stem from sexual trauma.

COMMON DREAM SYMBOLS

Snakes: Snakes in dreams have many meanings, and interpretations can vary. Sigmund Freud believed that snakes symbolise our sexual energy, the penis. He stated that male sexual symbols in dreams are snakes, reptiles and fish. Dreams about snakes relate to sexuality and male figures in life. They reflect one's experience of manhood. For women, snakes can symbolise relationships with men or male energy. Carl Jung said the most common dream symbol of transcendence is the snake. He said the unconscious mind speaks through images and symbols. They represent what is happening now and what may happen in the future (Kakunje et al., 2019).

Bees: Bees are an essential symbol in dreams and mythology. Many believe they are sacred. They connect the natural world to the underworld. Generally, bees in dreams signify good luck or a prosperous future. However, the specific context is crucial. *Were you attacked by bees? Did they sting you? Did you dream of bees and honey? Was it a bee or a wasp?*

Falling: Dreaming of falling often reflects fears about social failure. Barrett (2013) suggests asking further questions, such as: '*Did you lose balance? Were you pushed? Did you fall from a building, or was someone else falling?*' Each of these scenarios can alter the dream's interpretation.

Teeth Falling Out: Interpreting the common dream of teeth falling out can vary in different ways. Freud said dreams of teeth falling out reflect fears of castration or sexual repression. In modern views, it often symbolises a fear of one's appearance, embarrassment and ageing. Jung, on the other hand, saw it as a symbol of change. It meant losing old aspects of the self to make way for new growth.

Pregnancy: Dreams of pregnancy can symbolise creativity, growth and development. Jung viewed these dreams as indicating that something new is developing within the dreamer, such as a new idea, project or phase of life. It's a powerful symbol of potential and new beginnings.

Houses: Houses in dreams often represent the self or the dreamer's mind. Different rooms can symbolise various aspects of one's personality or other areas of life. For example, the attic might represent hidden thoughts or memories, while the basement could symbolise the subconscious or repressed emotions. Jung would look at the house as a whole and its connection to the dreamer's personal development and psyche.

As we can see, even though we may dream of a bee, snake or house, many different factors associated with these symbols are important to consider. We can identify the actual meaning by taking note of as much information as possible in our dreams. Between self-reflection and the dream's context, we can find the interpretation that resonates with us. Then, we can compare the interpretation to our actual lives to see if there are any relevant issues or inspirations for self-improvement.

Think of your dreams as a treasure chest of personal insights and growth. They can show you new ways to develop, heal and connect spiritually. So, when you next drift off to sleep, remember your dreams hold valuable messages. Embrace them, reflect on what they might be telling you and let them guide life's journey.

OUR PURPOSE IN LIFE

 'Your work is to discover your world and then with all your heart give yourself to it'. — Buddha

What is the *why* of our life?

We all may wonder why we're here on Earth. What made us come to this Earth, and what purpose do we have here?

What is the meaning and purpose of life? This is a very philosophical question. But is it only for philosophers? We all should ask ourselves this question, keeping in mind that the meaning and purpose of life differ for each person.

When we start asking these more profound questions, we evoke the significance of our existence. This is the fuel for activating purpose and motivation. This activation provides meaning and direction. When we align with our purpose, everything begins to fall into place. There can be more than one purpose, as it does not need to be restrictive.

Josh et al. (2023) and his team wrote the paper 'Scientific Philosophy'. It explores the philosophy behind the question, *Who am I?* The philosophy is about existence, metaphysics and ethics. They found that exploring a person's identity is individual and subjective. Our experiences, beliefs and values can define who we are. Our relationships with family, friends and coworkers will undoubtedly provide us with an identity. However, when we can answer with conviction, we know exactly who we are; this is true self-discovery.

Sometimes, we might really know our purpose but hold back because we're afraid of being laughed at. We might think another path seems better, even when our gut tells us otherwise. For me, writing this book is a great example of following my purpose.

Even though I've faced some mockery and scepticism, I trusted myself and my instincts. I believe that by writing this book, I'll ultimately be able to help others. Don't let anyone steer you away from your path if it feels right and your intuition backs it up. I cannot stress the word *trust* enough.

Some might argue we have no purpose but to exist and get through the day-to-day. I implore you to reconsider this. Living without a sense of meaning leads to a life filled with dissatisfaction, and the road is much more difficult.

We all live on this wonderful Earth, and having a purpose helps us enjoy every moment. Does lacking purpose bring joy, or are we constantly seeking the next thing to satisfy us? It's easy to feel negative when we're down and lose our sense of direction. Now is the time to reflect on our lives and rediscover our purpose.

Ask yourself: *Do I truly love what I do?* It is time to ignite your passion and identify what matters most. This is the key to creating meaningful differences in our lives and others. Choose a purpose with depth and significance, something that truly resonates with you and brings lasting fulfilment. The best thing is—we can have more than one!

Part of this questioning is like being a scientist, examining our hearts under a cosmic microscope.

Our days are too precious NOT to experience connection, rich meaning and purpose.

SO HOW DO WE RECOGNISE PURPOSE?

Purpose feels bigger than us; it gives us a sense of fulfilment and hope. As mentioned earlier in this book, purpose aligns us with our higher self. Purpose energises us, and we experience enthusiasm when we encounter it.

My purpose has always been the same—to help others. Yet the dynamics have changed as the years progress. I once had a purpose for myself and another for my business. My business purpose was to serve my clients in their business journey. As I evolved, my purpose grew. It became to serve others in their spiritual self-discovery. My purpose statement is now, *'I am committed to being a helping hand on your life journey. I will help you find your purpose and joy and live your best life'*.

When I was in business, I set up processes for clients to follow to help them achieve their goals. They knew what they wanted to achieve in their business but did not know how to get there or where to start. They needed help reaching that goal, maintaining it and setting new ones.

If they were starting a business, I asked them questions to spark ideas. The questions were about what they wanted to achieve and how they planned to do it. This led me to help them set up a path of steps and actions required to get there. Sometimes, there would be detours. We would need to add new steps or backtrack and make a new way. This was all a part of the road to fulfilment. At the end of this chapter, you will find some resources and helpful lists to help your thought processes.

WHAT ARE SOME WAYS WE CAN IDENTIFY AND FIND OUR
PURPOSE?

A Vision Board

A vision board is a great way to visualise finding your purpose. In the 'Manifestation' chapter, I have provided step-by-step instructions on how to make a vision board.

Gratitude

I love feeling gratitude. With gratitude, so many things come into alignment for us. Daily gratitude fills our lives with abundance. Joy and happiness come to us in small ways, and we may notice this once we start practising gratitude. Gratitude spurs on purpose and fuels all those feel-good chemicals in our system. The universe loves gratitude, too!

We explore this concept further in the chapter 'Gratitude'.

Join a Group

Another way to stimulate purpose is by joining a group. Joining a group of like-minded people can help us express ourselves. We do this by doing things we feel passionate about. Our group could be into stamp collecting. If seeing a rare stamp and talking about it with other group members excites us, this equals joy. Some might enjoy football, and in Australia, Aussie Rules football is extremely popular. Being part of a club with fellow members supporting our team when they win can make us feel exhilarated. When they lose, we have compatriots to sympathise with. However, we do it all in the name of support and being part of a community. Joining = connection = the pathway to purpose.

Turning Pain into Purpose

Sometimes, you may have had a traumatic event, and you can turn the pain into a purpose. This is one of life's true miracles of alchemy. When we witness someone who experiences a horrible event, heals, and then helps others, it is a wondrous thing to behold. To turn trauma into a purpose, first, you must recognise it. Then, you must overcome it so you can help others. As I mentioned in 'Remembering Who We Are', this is a challenging but highly rewarding path.

Doing Something We Love

Many people have passions like painting, sports, hiking and reading. There are so many opportunities out there that offer adventure and exploration!

Remember, you can have many interests in different areas, so why not try something new? It's easy to push aside hobbies because we succumb to the notion that we don't have time. Hobbies or spending time like this should be part of your self-care routine.

Make it a top priority to carve out time for what you love. When we bring some spark back into our lives—our body and mind will thank us for it.

Give Back

This is not just a gift of money. It can also be a gift of time. Time is precious for the charities or associations we are helping. Yet, I must say that giving our time to a cause gives us so much purpose as well. Time is valuable to all of us. Finding an association we can give to can mean a lot to the association, its members and the recipients. I have been part of various associations over the years, and it gives me great joy to give back. When my children were in kindergarten, I was the treasurer and made many changes that helped the kindergarten set up systems for future years.

I belonged to another association related to my work for many years. I would hold meetings to support other BAS agents and bookkeepers. We would explain the latest changes and discuss different topics that were important to members. Our industry was one where many worked alone. So, it was invaluable to provide support.

Developing our purpose is helpful, along with some of the tools mentioned above. Don't forget to use our intuition as a core tool as well. Writing down lists externalises our thoughts and is a beautiful reflection record. When thinking about what to do next, check to see if it aligns with our purpose.

ANALYSING YOUR JOY AND VALUE

What Brings You Joy and Value in Your Life Now?

- Focus on the positive aspects of your life you currently appreciate and cherish.
- Consider how these joys align with your core values and passions.

IDENTIFYING CHALLENGES

What's Making Your Life Difficult?

- List the things that are hard to deal with right now. Then, see what you can change.
- What steps can you take to eliminate the things making your life complicated?
- Can you break them down into smaller, more manageable steps?
- Remember, small changes can lead to significant improvements over time. Think of yourself as the gardener of your life:
- Which weeds need to go?
- Which areas of the garden need fertilising?

WORKING ON HABITS

Do You Have Habits That You Need to Change?

- Identify recurring habits that might be holding you back.
- Break down these habits and address them one step at a time.
- Understand that changing habits can be challenging because they are ingrained in your subconscious. Be patient and persistent.
- Consider replacing negative habits with positive ones that support your goals.

UNDERSTANDING YOUR PURPOSE

Why Do You Do What You Do?

- Reflect on the motivations behind your actions and decisions. Understanding your 'why' can provide clarity and direction.
- Connect your daily actions to your long-term goals and aspirations.

What's Your Purpose When You Get up Every Morning?

- Define the reason you wake up each day. This can help guide your actions and bring more meaning to your daily life.
- Ensure that your daily purpose aligns with your core values and long-term vision.

TAKING ACTION

Work on Each Item on This List.

- The goal is to reduce and eliminate the negatives, bringing you closer to growing the joyful parts of your life.
- Celebrate small victories and progress to stay motivated.

By breaking down your life into these lists and reflecting on each aspect, you can better understand what makes you happy and what needs to change. Remember, you have the power to cultivate your life, one small step at a time. Focus on growth, and be kind to yourself throughout the journey.

LEAVE YOUR EGO AT THE DOOR

 'The ego is not master in its own house'. — Sigmund Freud

Ego. It's a small word with a big impact, but we must go there! Dwayne Johnson once said, '*Check your ego at the door. The ego can be a great success inhibitor. It can kill opportunities, and it can kill success*'. It's hard for many to balance the ego's complexities. It forms our identity. We must trust ourselves and our abilities. But we must not let our ego get in the way.

Psychologists have extensively explored the concept of the ego. Walsh et al. (1980) describe the ego as encompassing the roles, self-images and analytical aspects of our minds with which we usually identify. This explores classical psychoanalysis, which presents two versions of the ego. The first is the strong ego, which is considered a hallmark of health and assists in everyday functions. The second is the transpersonal perspective. It sees the ego as an illusion, a product of distorted perception. Awakening occurs when we sever ties with our ego-based identity. It offers freedom and empowerment.

A healthy ego is crucial to some extent, but at what point does it become detrimental? When does the ego start to get in the way? Think about why we may seek approval from others. Does it add any real value to our lives, or is it just a perceived value, making you feel superior or equal to others? A person with an inflated ego can be difficult to be around because they lack empathy, always needing to be right and dismissing opinions as unimportant.

Our ego can drive that inner voice. When we feel inferior, this voice often turns into negative self-talk. We don't need to be narcissistic or egotistical to have an ego issue. The ego can be very self-deprecating, constantly comparing us to others, seeking perfectionism and worrying about how we are perceived. These aspects can hinder our spiritual journey and stop us from experiencing the beautiful awakening of freedom and purpose.

Walsh et al. (1980) noted that attachment is not limited to external objects or people. We can be equally attached to a particular self-image, behaviour pattern or psychological process. Among the strongest attachments are those to suffering and unworthiness. We often believe our identity is derived from our roles, problems, relationships or the contents of consciousness, reinforcing attachment through fear of personal survival. *'If I give up my attachments, who and what will I be?'*

THE AWARE FORMULA FOR SPOTTING EGO INFLUENCE

To help you notice when your ego is influencing your behaviour, I came up with the AWARE formula:

A – Assess Your Thoughts and Feelings

Ask yourself: *Am I feeling defensive, superior or inferior?*

Look for thoughts about seeking validation, comparing yourself to others or proving yourself.

W – Why Am I Reacting?

What is the source of your actions or reactions? Question: Is your response driven by fear, insecurity or a need for approval?

A – Align with Your True Self

Check in with yourself and ask if your actions and thoughts align with your values and authentic self. Determine if you act out of genuine intention or if your ego is steering the wheel.

R – Recognise and Reframe

Recognise ego-driven patterns and reframe them with a more balanced perspective. Replace thoughts like *'I need to be right'* with *'I value other perspectives'*.

E – Empathy and Connection

Practice empathy by considering others' feelings and viewpoints. Refocus on building connections rather than seeking validation or superiority.

WAYS TO LET GO OF YOUR EGO

You might wonder if it's possible to let go of the ego. The answer is yes, it is possible.

Here are some practical ways to do so:

Dance: Dancing like nobody's watching lets us express ourselves. It releases dopamine and lifts our mood, free from judgement. This can be scary for some of us, but once we release the attachment of judgement, bring on the liberation!

Compliments: A genuine compliment shifts our focus from ourselves to others, helping us appreciate them. This practice fosters humility and connection. Instead of seeking validation, we can provide it, reducing ego-driven thoughts. Complimenting others lifts their spirits. It also reminds them to celebrate the strengths of others, as discussed in the chapter 'Gratitude'.

Go out in nature: Connecting with nature reduces ego-driven thoughts and grounds you. Refer to the chapters 'Nature' and 'Water H_2O'.

Let go of anger: Anger often stems from fear. Processing anger lets us see other views and reduces ego-driven reactions. Instead of responding defensively, we can respond with curiosity. We can ask ourselves why we feel angry and what the other person's perspective might be. This approach builds understanding and empathy and reduces the ego's hold.

Gratitude: Practising gratitude shifts our focus from what we lack to what we have. By regularly expressing gratitude, we can reduce feelings of envy and comparison, which are often driven by the ego. We discuss this further in the chapter 'Gratitude'.

Meditate: Mindfulness and meditation help overcome ego attachments. The chapter 'Meditation' delves into mindfulness practices.

Being vulnerable: Embrace vulnerability by being honest and open with ourselves and others. This keeps the ego in check.

Stop and think about what you say: Consider if your words add value or show a need to dominate. Listening to others is key. Don't forget our section about active listening in the 'Gratitude' chapter!

Why do you do what you do: Evaluate if your actions align with your values and bring you happiness. Are you creating a dynamic that no longer serves you? Are old beliefs keeping you in a stagnant loop? The chapter 'Our Purpose in Life' explores this question. It helps you see if your work brings you fulfilment.

Mindfulness and meditation: Become aware of our thoughts and feelings without getting attached to them. Regular practice can help us see our ego from a distance and reduce its influence on our behaviour. Techniques like breath focus, body scanning or guided meditations can help.

Self-Inquiry: This involves asking deep, reflective questions. They help us understand the root causes of our ego-driven behaviours. Questions like *'Who am I without my achievements?'* or *'What am I trying to prove?'* can help us uncover the insecurities driving our ego.

Service to others: Volunteering can shift our focus from our own needs. Acts of kindness can reduce the ego's grip. They foster a sense of connection and empathy with others.

Practice humility: Humility means knowing our limits and accepting that we are not always right. We can do this by acknowledging our mistakes, seeking feedback and valuing others' strengths.

Journaling: Writing our thoughts and feelings helps us see ego-driven patterns. Reflecting on our egos can help us be more selfless. A short daily journal of our intentions keeps the ego at bay and helps us focus on what truly matters.

Embrace failure and learn from it: Mistakes are okay. See failures as chances to grow, not threats to your self-worth. Embracing failure helps break down the ego's need for perfection and control.

Foster deep connections: Deep, meaningful relationships can help us transcend ego-driven, superficial interactions. Authentic connections are not about competition or validation. They rely on mutual respect, understanding and empathy.

Adopt a growth mindset: Focus on learning and growth, not fixed traits. This view urges us to see challenges as growth opportunities. It lessens the ego's need for constant validation and success.

Letting go of the ego allows our true, authentic selves to emerge. We become more compassionate, calm and confident, no longer needing others' approval. Embracing this change can lead to a more fulfilling and balanced life. Hanging up the ego at the door is when our true, authentic selves come into the vision. We have compassion for others, and calmness will surround us.

By understanding and embracing the role of the ego, we can navigate its challenges and use it as a tool for personal growth and self-actualisation. Remember, the ego can be both an obstacle and a teacher. Recognise its presence, understand its influence and allow it to guide you towards a deeper understanding of yourself and your potential.

EMOTIONS AND AILMENTS

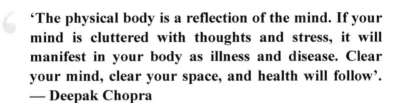

 'The physical body is a reflection of the mind. If your
mind is cluttered with thoughts and stress, it will
manifest in your body as illness and disease. Clear
your mind, clear your space, and health will follow'.
— Deepak Chopra

Our mental, emotional and physical states are so closely tied that they
create a constant feedback loop. On the path to self-actualisation, we
must remain conscious and self-aware of our emotions—understanding
why we have them, what triggers them and how we can learn from and
regulate them. Often, our feelings and emotional reactions become
second nature, influencing every action in our lives. If left unprocessed, these emotions can dominate us, leading to stress and potentially causing physical ailments. They become beliefs, then internal
facts, creating a distorted lens through which we see the world.

When something happens, how do we react? There is joy, happiness,
excitement and sometimes tears when something positive happens. We
emit positive energy and excitement around us, radiating this vibration.

Our faces may shine with a smile from ear to ear, and there's a spring in our step.

What happens when we see something as negative or terrible? Our shoulders slump, and we may experience fear, rage or shame. If the situation is extreme, our body may release high levels of cortisol, and we can experience panic.

Our emotions greatly impact our physical health, and it all starts with the limbic system in our brain. This system includes the hypothalamus, thalamus, amygdala and hippocampus. The hippocampus creates long-term memories and stores them in our brains. The amygdala will see those memories and attach emotions associated with them. That's why certain smells or songs can bring back strong emotional memories.

LET'S LOOK AT THE SCIENCE

Hormonal Response

When we feel emotions, our bodies release hormones like adrenaline and cortisol. These hormones help us deal with stress by preparing our body for a fight-or-flight reaction. This is useful in short bursts, but if we're stressed for a long time, too much cortisol can harm our bodies. High levels of cortisol can weaken our immune system, raise blood pressure and lead to anxiety and depression.

Neurotransmitters

Neurotransmitters are chemical messengers in the brain that play a crucial role in transmitting signals between nerve cells, or neurons, as well as from neurons to other types of cells. We are focusing on serotonin and dopamine. These also play a role in our moods and emotions. Both dopamine and serotonin are called the 'feel-good' neurotransmitters. Serotonin is crucial for keeping our mood balanced and is primarily produced in our gut. Low levels of serotonin are linked to depression and anxiety. Dopamine is another crucial neurotransmitter that deals with pleasure and reward. When dopamine levels are off, it can affect our motivation and enjoyment of life.

Gut-Brain Axis

The gut-brain axis connects our emotions and gut health. Our gut, sometimes called the 'second brain', has many neurons and produces neurotransmitters like serotonin. The vagus nerve is involved in this two-way communication system between the gut and the brain. Most of our serotonin is made in the gut, which shows how important gut health is for our emotional well-being. Understanding this connection reminds us to take care of our physical and emotional health.

Now that we understand the science behind our emotions, we can consider the next step: making choices. We have a few options—we can ignore our emotions, be curious about them or deny them altogether.

When we ignore our emotions by stuffing them down or bottling them up, we paradoxically let them rule our lives. Ignoring them can harm our physical and mental health. The body becomes out of tune and out of alignment because the emotion is sitting in our body, causing stress and imbalance.

Conversely, curiosity about our emotions can help us better understand and manage them more healthily. This means taking the time to notice how we feel, asking ourselves why we feel that way and figuring out what we can do to address those feelings.

Denying our emotions means refusing to acknowledge them at all. This can lead to even more significant problems because those emotions don't just disappear—they build up. They can eventually cause more serious physical and mental health issues.

Our choices can manifest in a variety of ways.

One of the most fundamental aspects of the human experience is free will, which means the free will to choose. When we exercise our free will, we possess a sense of agency.

We have a choice in how we view an experience.

We have a choice to learn about our emotions and the resulting impact. This can be confronting, but it is essential to be aware of the self, a.k.a. self-awareness, and how these choices shape our reality.

What might this look like? Let's say my computer system crashed on Saturday, and I have an urgent project due on Monday. I checked everything and could not find the problem. So what are my choices?

1. After the initial shock, I can view this as a negative addition to my life and say, *'Why now? Why me? Why does this always happen to me?'* Rabbit hole incoming!
2. I could acknowledge, *'Ok, this is out of my control'*, and ask, *'What can I learn from this? How can I make this better? Did this happen to teach me something? If so, what is it?'* From a practical level, perhaps if we added new procedures around this event, this problem could be avoided in the future.
3. Could the computer crash be viewed as a blessing or benefit? Receiving this now on Saturday gives me time to sort things out, and it would have been worse receiving this on Monday. Maybe I wasn't paying attention to an alert on the computer because I was so stressed and focused on finishing I wasn't mindful of my process. Or perhaps I needed the pause to stop, breathe and chill out. This isn't the end of the world. So, I will breathe, not think in worst-case scenarios and just pause.

Note: Often, when this happens, a solution can magically appear, or the issue resolves itself. Interesting, right?

Acknowledging our emotions and how to master them can help, too. Let's paint another scenario. We have argued with a family member over something that was said. Here is what we can do:

1. **Stop:** Stop and assess what has happened. We can give our

brains a moment to digest what is going on. We do not judge ourselves or add extra pressure.

2. **Acknowledge:** Acknowledge the feelings and the emotions. Are they positive or negative? Are we resisting those feelings or accepting that it is what it is? Have we reacted out loud, or have we internalised the emotion?

3. **Explore:** Exploring our emotions cannot be underestimated. We have acknowledged that we have, for example, felt sadness, anger and disappointment over an argument. If we have reacted poorly and out of character, this can be the time to examine the trigger of so much anger. Has this brought out memories that are painful as this has happened again? Did it bring out feelings of not being good enough and not being valued?

4. **Action:** Come up with an action plan to move forward. What can we learn from this situation? How can we overcome the feelings that have been brought forward? This is the time to make new plans and put them into action. We can express gratitude that these feelings have come up so they can be healed.

5. **Review:** Review the plans and strategies we have put into action previously and change anything that is no longer serving us, and if this is the case, then release it.

Below is another example that is fictional, but it is another scenario that can happen. While not every physical condition is caused by psychological factors, science shows us that the mind and body are inextricably linked. Psychological factors can significantly influence physical health, and physical conditions can, in turn, impact our mental state. The connection works both ways, highlighting the profound interrelationship between mind and body in overall well-being.

Example: Petra is experiencing bullying at her workplace. A colleague is being deliberately toxic, and she feels anxious about going to work. Petra tells herself not to be silly and to get on with it, pushing her feelings down. So, she soldiers on. But the bullying continues, and within a few months, Petra starts to suffer from a sore stomach and reflux, which eventually develops into a stomach ulcer. Petra has been ignoring her emotions. Instead, she could have chosen to be curious about her anxiety and her relationship with the bully, understanding her emotional triggers and why she felt uncomfortable confronting the situation. Where did this fear come from?

If Petra had explored these questions, she might have prevented the excessive buildup of stomach acid, understood the nature of her anxiety and managed or resolved it—an empowering act. She might have even advocated for herself, interrupting the bully's negative impact. Most importantly, she wouldn't have suppressed her emotions and prevented them from worsening.

Of course, there are many ways this fictional situation could have played out differently. Petra shouldn't be hard on herself; we humans often do this without even realising it. This is one of the reasons I felt so compelled to write this book. By opening our eyes and hearts to this information, we can move into a more beautiful, purposeful and happier life.

Another example: Do you have a sore back? This may mean that you do not feel supported in what you do.

It is our choice whether to listen to our ailment, as there is a reason for the persistent sore throat or back pain. Do we have a lesson to learn, but we are not paying attention to what is already there? This is tough love from our bodies that demands our attention.

It can be very challenging to think clearly when we're experiencing pain and suffering. It's easy to fall into a rabbit hole of negative thoughts, but this is counterproductive. While it might seem like the easy option, easy doesn't always mean right. When we go down that rabbit hole, it can be challenging to climb back out, preventing us from fully embracing our lives.

Negative emotions create blockages, sidetrack and imprison us in a cycle of negativity. This distraction makes it hard to focus on regaining our sense of agency and positivity and finding solutions to improve our circumstances. By shifting our focus towards self-compassion and positive thinking, we can break free from these negative patterns and start making meaningful changes in our lives.

Some people might equate self-compassion with feeling sorry for themselves, but feeling empathy for our experiences is an act of self-care and self-love. Understand that going down a rabbit hole of negativity differs from losing self-compassion. While it's important to acknowledge our feelings, it's equally important to avoid ruminating on negative thoughts and instead remain fluid in our emotional responses.

Positive thought reduces disease. According to findings from Johns Hopkins expert Lisa R. Yanek, MPH, people with a family history of heart disease who also had a positive outlook were one-third less likely to have a heart attack or other cardiovascular event within five to twenty-five years than those with a more negative outlook.

According to a study by Caprara et al. (2017), positivity can be a significant psychological asset, helping individuals view life with a positive outlook. The immune systems of those with high levels of positivity respond better to stress. The study highlights that individual differences in personality traits, self-beliefs, attitudes and habits can influence health and well-being. This growing body of research suggests that personality, as a self-regulating system, is crucial in promoting health and moderating vulnerability to adversities and illnesses. There are countless more studies completed to support this evidence.

According to a study titled 'Understanding Mind-Body Interaction from the Perspective of East Asian Medicine' (Lee, 2017), emotions are believed to be held in specific organs. The study found that 'Anger is associated with the liver, happiness with the heart, thoughtfulness with the heart and spleen, sadness with the heart and lungs, fear with the kidneys and the heart, surprise with the heart and the gallbladder, and anxiety with the heart and the lungs'. This research provides a fascinating insight into the connection between our emotions and physical health.

When we look at the science and all the feelings involved and dig into the mind-body connection, you could say that having a positive mindset and being self-aware is essentially taking preventive health action. Conversely, when we don't endeavour to understand the connection, our health can be negatively impacted.

I often think about how society tells us we must always be prim, proper and in control as if that's the true sign of resilience. But this couldn't be further from the truth. What if a major event happens in our lives, like the passing of a beloved family member? We're told to be strong and hold it together. You might hear people say, *'Oh, they were so strong!'* as a compliment. However, I've realised that this isn't healthy for us. Why are we told to stifle our emotions?

It is necessary for us to feel and express our emotions, both the good and the bad. If we feel like crying, why can't we cry? Why are we holding back? I've observed, particularly in Western society, that we condition ourselves to be strong by swallowing our feelings and keeping them hidden. But true resilience comes from allowing ourselves to feel and express those emotions, not bottling them up. When we give ourselves permission to feel and process an emotion, we feel relieved and lighter.

SOME METHODS TO HELP YOU RELEASE

Screaming or roaring in public isn't welcomed in most places, and let's face it, extreme public emotion is something the world might not be ready for just yet. So, we can go home, shut the doors and windows and scream at the top of our lungs, or do it in the car where no one will hear us. This is known as a primal release. We might feel tired afterwards due to the expulsion of so much energy, but we can feel much lighter. We can even try setting a clock for a 5-10 minute daily release in a private space where we allow ourselves to express ourselves however we please.

In addition to the suggestions above, you can also utilise the tools in Part Two of this book to assist in emotional healing. Here's how we might combine those different methods to navigate your emotions and clear blockages:

Sound Healing

A wonderful way to start is by humming or singing our favourite song. Let yourself dance and feel the joy that comes from singing. If you need to sing a song of heartbreak, do it. This can help you release your feelings, allowing the anger or sadness to slowly subside. Humming and singing act as forms of sound healing.

Sound bowls are another fantastic tool. The 'Chakra' chapter provides information on sound frequencies and healing techniques. The vibrations from the bowls can help clear emotional blockages and restore balance.

Writing Down Your Feelings

Journaling is a powerful way to process emotions. Writing down our feelings helps us to think about the situation and the accompanying emotions. It gives us time to reflect on why we feel a certain way and consider how we can make changes to shift that emotion. Keeping a journal allows us to track our feelings over time, revealing patterns that might emerge. If we notice a recurring pattern, it's important to break it by addressing the root of the issue.

Meditation and Mindfulness

After journaling, we might choose to meditate on the emotions we have identified. Meditation creates space for emotions to surface and helps us to reflect on them more clearly. Nature can be an excellent setting for mindfulness, offering a calming environment to explore our feelings. Practising gratitude and manifestation can further help express emotions and enhance self-awareness.

Clearing Your Space and Energy

Finally, clearing our physical space and energy can help release and clear emotional blockages. Decluttering our environment and using techniques like smudging or energy healing can create a more positive and supportive atmosphere for emotional healing.

By combining these tools from Part Two, we can develop a comprehensive approach to emotional healing, which can help us navigate and release blockages effectively.

Tuning Fork Therapy

We can practise tuning fork therapy on ourselves. Still, it is much easier when someone else facilitates, or we can practise it with friends and family. It involves a series of different-sized tuning forks with two steel prongs that vibrate at various levels when placed at different parts of the body. They can help alleviate muscular and bone pain. Some frequencies vibrate at a level that can bring more love and joy as they vibrate at such a high level, bringing a more spiritual influence over the use of the tuning fork. Various practitioners use tuning forks for healing.

EFT Tapping

EFT (Emotional Freedom Techniques) tapping is a powerful tool for emotional release. It combines ancient Chinese acupressure and modern psychology. The practice involves tapping specific body meridian points and focusing on one particular issue or emotion. This can help to release blocked energy and reduce emotional distress. EFT tapping helps to balance the body's energy system by stimulating specific points. It often provides immediate relief from negative emotions like anxiety, stress and anger.

You can either engage a trained EFT tapping practitioner or learn the technique yourself.

Acupuncture

Over the years, I have found this method very useful in treating so many different ailments.

Acupuncture is a traditional Chinese medicine practice. It involves inserting thin needles into specific points on the body. This stimulates energy flow and promotes healing. This ancient technique is based on the concept of Qi (pronounced 'chee'), which is the life force energy that flows through pathways in the body called meridians. When Qi is blocked or imbalanced, it can lead to physical and emotional ailments.

Acupuncture aims to restore the flow of Qi. It helps with health issues, including emotional stress. Acupuncture can improve emotional well-being by releasing pent-up emotions and reducing stress, anxiety and depression. It boosts the body's healing powers and supports the mind-body link.

A licensed practitioner usually administers acupuncture. They tailor the treatment to your needs. Sessions can be deeply relaxing. They relieve emotional and physical tension. Many find that regular acupuncture helps their emotional balance and health.

Kinesiology

Kinesiology is a holistic therapy that uses gentle muscle testing to assess the body's imbalances and emotional blockages. It operates on the principle that our muscles are linked to our body's energy pathways. By testing these muscles, a kinesiologist can find stress and imbalances. The goal is to correct these imbalances and promote emotional and physical well-being.

In a kinesiology session, the practitioner asks you to hold a position. Then, they apply light pressure to a muscle. The muscle's response provides information about the state of your body and mind. If the muscle is weak or gives way, it indicates an imbalance or blockage. The kinesiologist then uses various techniques to help restore balance. These include acupressure, massage and nutritional advice.

Kinesiology can help with emotional release by identifying and addressing underlying issues. Balancing the body's energy systems can help reduce stress, anxiety and other negative emotions. You can work with a trained kinesiologist. They will guide you and provide treatments based on your needs. Many find kinesiology a gentle yet powerful way to release deep emotions. It brings a greater sense of balance and harmony to their lives.

Somatic Movement or Somatic Dance Movement Classes

Somatic movement and dance classes focus on the body's internal sensations. They aim to heal emotionally and physically. These classes stress mindfulness and body awareness by helping people connect with their bodies and release stored tension and emotions.

Somatic movement involves gentle, mindful exercises that enhance body awareness and promote relaxation. These movements help us listen to our body, understand its signals and restore balance and harmony. The practice urges us to move slowly and with intent, focusing on how our body feels and where we might hold tension.

Somatic movement, through guided exercises, can release blockages. It promotes well-being and a mind-body connection. It's beneficial for those with chronic pain, stress or trauma. It provides a safe space to explore and heal these issues.

Somatic dance movement merges bodily movement with the freedom of dance. These classes often involve improvisation, allowing us to move in a way that feels natural and authentic. It focuses on the internal experience, not the external form. So, it is accessible to all, regardless of dance experience.

Yoga

Yoga is an ancient practice. It originated in India and had roots in Hindu, Buddhist and Jain traditions. It involves moving energy around the body. It does this through a mix of physical postures (asanas), breathing exercises (pranayama) and meditation. Yoga is now a popular worldwide exercise and health practice. It offers many benefits, such as improved flexibility, strength and balance. It also boosts mental clarity, reduces stress and enhances well-being. It aims to harmonise the body, mind and spirit. Its holistic approach promotes balance within the individual.

- Bikram Yoga: also known as hot yoga, is practised in heated rooms. The temperature is typically set to around 105°F (40°C) with 40 per cent humidity. This heat warms our muscles. It allows a deeper stretch and greater flexibility. Bikram yoga uses a specific series of twenty-six postures and breathing exercises. They are performed in the same sequence. The heat and the sequence will work the whole body. They provide a complete workout and help detoxify. It's intense but can be incredibly rewarding.
- Hatha Yoga: a gentle, slow-paced form of yoga. It's perfect for beginners or those wanting a more relaxed practice. It involves a combination of meditation, physical poses (asanas) and breathing exercises (pranayama). I have practised Hatha yoga for many years and find it very relaxing. It helps me maintain my flexibility and provides a calming balance to my day. Hatha yoga classes focus on basic postures and alignment. They provide a solid foundation for yoga beginners.
- Ashtanga Yoga: a more vigorous and physically demanding form of Hatha yoga. It consists of six levels (or series) of postures, each increasing in difficulty. The practice is known for its dynamic, flowing movements. They are synchronised with breath (vinyasa). Each series must be mastered before

moving on to the next, ensuring a progressive buildup of strength, flexibility and stamina. Ashtanga yoga needs dedication and consistency. It can be gratifying for those who enjoy a challenging practice.

This book draws from many ancient practices, recognising the wisdom and effectiveness of traditions that have stood the test of time. For centuries, cultures worldwide have understood the profound connection between mind, body and spirit, incorporating holistic practices into their daily lives to promote health and well-being. However, the Western world has been slower in adopting these holistic approaches, often favouring conventional medicine and technological advancements over ancient wisdom.

Today, we are witnessing a significant shift. There is a growing acceptance of ancient spiritual practices. These include meditation, yoga, acupuncture and herbal medicine. These practices are becoming popular and are being rigorously tested. Researchers are finding out how they work, and these findings support what many have long believed.

This convergence of ancient wisdom and modern science marks an exciting era of awakening. People are more open to using these old practices. They see their value in promoting holistic health. As science explores and validates these practices, collective consciousness is rising. We are also learning how connected our physical, mental and spiritual selves are.

The vibrations of this shift are palpable, signalling a move towards a more holistic and enlightened approach to health and life.

By expressing what we need, our body will thank us. Our body will not be festering with emotion. IT WILL BE RELEASED. I cannot stress enough how important this is to our well-being.

We all came into this three-dimensional world to feel emotions, so we must acknowledge what we are feeling and then LET IT GO. By doing so, our whole body dynamics will change. We learn, and better yet, if we learn from an experience, it becomes valuable, which is true alchemy. If we don't learn from it, we propagate a loop, and the experience will repeat in different forms until we become the student.

Note: When suffering from mental and physical ailments, seek professional medical advice.

PART III
JOURNEYS OF THE HEART AND MIND

Welcome to Part Three: Journeys of the Heart and Mind. Here we will explore the intricacies of growth, the interlinking of relationships and the trials and tribulations that come along for the ride of the human experience.

How do the past, present and future interact, and how do our experiences from the past affect our present and future? This section provides valuable information from some of the world's leading trauma experts.

We will also discuss how reality and time perception relate to our healing process. Even the deep subject of crossing over will be covered, along with viewpoints on how these changes impact our own development.

Consider this section a supportive area where we investigate the intricacies of recovery and the significant influence of relationships in our lives. Every chapter will give you knowledge and skills to help you heal and build stronger relationships, creating conditions for a happier, more balanced existence.

Be sure to use the tools in Part Two as a vehicle to help you better understand and activate your journey in a positive and healing way.

TRAUMA

 **'The wound is the place where the Light enters you'.
— Rumi**

Trauma brings a complexity that can profoundly impact our lives. When left unresolved, the cascading negative impact on our human experience can be quite tragic. Trauma can be so deeply rooted that it can subconsciously alter our perceptions of the world and the people in it. It can deeply wound but is also a sneaky companion. Some of us know we have trauma, while for others, its impact may be hidden from our conscious decisions, thoughts and ideas. Our responses and every interaction we have can be shaped by trauma.

But what is it exactly? People often associate trauma with a car accident or a physical dramatic event that leaves a scar. The Oxford Dictionary describes trauma as a deeply distressing or disturbing event, such as losing a child or a physical accident. However, in recent years, in the mental health space, trauma has been deeply explored, and we now know so much more.

Trauma can be broadly defined as experiences that cause intense physical and psychological stress reactions. This can be in one event or complex trauma, where the event continues over some time in combination with other traumatic events. In extreme cases of stress trauma, the trauma overwhelms an individual's ability to cope, which may lead to symptoms of post-traumatic stress disorder (PTSD), including intrusive memories, avoidance behaviours and hyperarousal. (Chu et al., 2024)

In Australia, trauma is a significant concern, affecting a large portion of the population. The Australian Institute of Health and Welfare estimates that 75 per cent of Australian adults have experienced a traumatic event at some point in their lives.

More specifically, the National Study of Mental Health and Well-Being (2020–2022) reports that approximately 11 per cent of Australians experience PTSD in their lifetime. Women are nearly twice as likely to develop PTSD compared to men, with 14 per cent of women and 8 per cent of men affected.

Mental health conditions related to trauma are prevalent. The Australian Bureau of Statistics highlights that 26 per cent of Australians aged fifteen and over reported having a mental illness during the 2022 survey period. This includes conditions like depression and anxiety, which are often exacerbated by traumatic experiences.

When we leave trauma unresolved, it does indeed become a severe blockage. It prevents us from authentically experiencing life, holding us prisoner to past events. Despite the pain and disruption trauma brings, it also holds a gift for profound transformation. This sounds ridiculous, right? How can something that has had a terrible impact become a treasure? Healing from trauma invites us to face our deepest wounds, fostering resilience, compassion and a renewed sense of purpose. Often, through these challenging experiences, we uncover our true selves, developing deeper connections, self-compassion and meaning for ourselves and the world. Something awful that happened to us in the past does not belong to us and simply does not deserve to be a stowaway in our mind, body and spirit.

I am not an expert on trauma. However, I felt it was an intrinsic part of our journey in this book. Therefore, I have provided information about some of the world's leading experts in the field of trauma so that you might reflect more on its nature and consider how you might approach healing your trauma. Their publications are listed at the end of this book for easy reference.

Judith Lewis Herman

Judith Lewis Herman is an American psychiatrist who has revolutionised the field of trauma with her seminal book *Trauma and Recovery*. This work provides a foundational understanding of trauma's impact. It has been a cornerstone resource for both practitioners and survivors.

Herman emphasises the importance of dissociation and repressed memories; she asserts that remembering and processing traumatic events are crucial for recovery. She believes that knowledge and understanding play vital roles in the healing process.

Herman defines trauma as events that overwhelm the ordinary systems of care that give people a sense of control, connection and meaning. These events are extraordinary not because they are rare but because they exceed the human capacity to adapt. Trauma can shatter one's sense of self and the world, leading to feelings of helplessness, isolation and a profound loss of trust, deeply affecting identity and relationships.

Herman's extensive study of complex trauma, particularly from prolonged exposure to events like childhood abuse and domestic violence, led her to identify and describe complex PTSD (C-PTSD). This condition may present symptoms like difficulties with emotional regulation, changes in consciousness, negative self-perception and relationship challenges.

Gabor Maté

Dr Gabor Maté is a physician, speaker and author. His work on trauma has greatly impacted psychology and medicine. He takes a holistic approach. He stresses the link between mind, body and environment in healing trauma.

Maté considers the root causes of trauma and its manifestations in various aspects of life. He supports healing practices that are compassionate and integrative. Trauma creates lasting, heightened stress in the body. It affects the nervous system and causes health issues.

One of Maté's key messages is that trauma cannot always be conquered or resolved, but it can be acknowledged, held and loved. This perspective shifts the focus from trying to 'fix' trauma to understanding and compassionately engaging with it, allowing for a more profound healing process.

Peter Levine

Dr Peter Levine is known for developing somatic experiencing (SE). It is a body-focused approach to trauma healing. He defines trauma as a body response to overwhelming events. They are unprocessed and unintegrated. Trauma, stored in the body, harms physical and mental health.

Levine views trauma as a common human experience, not a pathological condition. He believes that recognising this normalises the experience and reduces stigma.

According to Levine, trauma occurs when the body's natural response to a threat (fight-or-flight) becomes 'stuck', leaving the individual unable to complete the necessary actions to defend themselves. This stuck energy continues to affect the individual long after the event has passed.

Somatic experience helps release trapped energy and restore balance to the nervous system. Levine's approach highlights the body's innate ability to heal and the importance of addressing the physiological aspects of trauma.

Bessel van der Kolk

Dr Bessel van der Kolk, a psychiatrist, integrates neuroscience, developmental psychology and body-centred therapies to understand and treat trauma. His book, *The Body Keeps the Score*, is a landmark in trauma studies, emphasising the synchronistic impact of trauma on the mind and body. Van der Kolk defines trauma as an experience that overwhelms an individual's capacity to cope, leaving a lasting impact on their psychological and physiological state. Traumatic experiences disrupt brain areas involved in memory, emotion regulation and the stress response, leading to symptoms like flashbacks, hypervigilance and emotional numbness.

He advocates for a holistic treatment approach that addresses both the mind and body. Van der Kolk supports body-oriented therapies. These include yoga, somatic experiencing and EMDR (Eye Movement Desensitisation and Reprocessing). They help people reconnect with their bodies and process trauma.

He also emphasises the importance of supportive relationships and the brain's ability to heal through neuroplasticity, highlighting the need for diverse therapeutic methods.

Richard C. Schwartz

Dr Richard C. Schwartz developed the Internal Family Systems (IFS) model. It is a unique approach to trauma therapy. The IFS model sees the mind as made of parts. Each part has its own traits and roles. Trauma often creates internal conflicts among these parts.

Schwartz Identifies Three Main Parts:

- **Exiles**: vulnerable parts that hold pain, fear and trauma, often suppressed due to their distressing nature

- **Managers**: protective parts that organise daily life to avoid triggering the exiles, manifesting as critical inner voices or perfectionistic behaviours
- **Firefighters:** reactive parts that distract exiles from their pain. They do this through impulsive or destructive behaviours.

The IFS model centres on the self. It is calm, curious, compassionate and confident. In a healthy mind, the self leads and unites the parts. It promotes healing and balance. IFS therapy helps individuals find their self. It builds compassion for their parts. This can heal and integrate inner conflicts.

Daniel Amen

Dr Daniel Amen, a psychiatrist and brain health expert, has significantly influenced the understanding and treatment of trauma through his innovative use of brain imaging. He has a large presence on social media, and many celebrities have sung his praises. He founded Amen Clinics, which uses SPECT (Single Photon Emission Computed Tomography) scans to evaluate brain function and develop targeted treatment plans. His work is ground-breaking and has redefined many pathologies involving the brain. SPECT imaging has changed diagnosis across the board and is a powerful tool.

Amen's approach emphasises brain health, integrating medical, psychological and lifestyle interventions to address the effects of trauma. His treatment plans often mix medication, therapy, nutrition, exercise and supplements. They aim to treat the whole person.

Amen has raised awareness of brain health through his books and talks. His work has made complex neuroscience concepts accessible. It has improved the understanding and management of trauma-related mental health issues.

Each of these experts (and so many more) offers unique insights and methods that can help create a personalised approach to healing from trauma. Trauma is multifaceted, and I believe it is an important aspect of our human condition we all need to explore.

Use the intentions and tools we've discussed in Part Two to tap into your intuition when deciding the best way to explore and heal your trauma. Trust yourself to know what feels right and be open to the journey ahead. Your path to healing is uniquely yours, and by listening to your inner guidance and experts trained extensively in trauma resolution or healing, you can find the approach that truly resonates with you. Remember, healing is a personal journey, and you've got the wisdom within to choose the way forward.

Note: Always seek the advice of qualified health providers with any questions regarding a medical or psychological condition.

TIME

 'Begin at once to live and count each separate day as a separate life'. — Seneca

'The more you think and worry about time, the more you will be controlled by it, and the faster it will appear to pass. The less you concern yourself with time, the freer you become, and there is always plenty of time'. — Scott Shaw in *Zen O'Clock: Time to Be.*

Savour each moment. It's challenging to believe that we all need to love each moment. We often feel bound by time, tracking every second, minute and hour as they turn into days. Imagine a life unrestricted by the constraints of time. Without the constant pressure of the next minute, how would your world transform?

Opening our minds to perceptions around time is crucial to self-actualisation.

If we are doing something we do not like, it can feel like time drags on forever. If you have ever been in an accident or a traumatic event, it can feel like time slows right down. Conversely, you may have heard the saying, *'Time flies when you're having fun!'* This illustrates how our perception of time relates to our experiences and emotions. When we are engaged and enjoying ourselves, time seems to move faster, but during unpleasant or stressful situations, it appears to slow down.

Albert Einstein was rumoured to have said, '*When you sit with a nice girl for two hours, you think it's only a minute, but when you sit on a hot stove for a minute, you think it's two hours. That's relativity*'.

We create every millisecond of our lives, and we are responsible for what is in front of us. We must know that we can change everything or nothing. It is all our choice.

WHAT IS THE DIFFERENCE BETWEEN A CHOICE AND A DECISION?

Every day, we are presented with choices that lead to decisions. Finding our purpose in life must be a conscious decision, not a passive choice or a default mechanism because our purpose influences all aspects of our lives.

Choice

A choice is a precursor to decision-making. We choose what food we eat and what clothes we wear. We must be free to make choices in our lives to make decisions. The opportunities that present themselves normally present themselves in choice first, and then the decision can be made.

THE PROCESS OF MAKING DECISIONS AND CHOICES

1. **Identify the problem**: Determine what decision needs to be made.
2. **Research**: Gather all relevant information and consider alternative solutions.
3. **Identify the options**: List all possible choices. Evaluate the suitability of each option.

4. **Make the choice**: Decide on the best option based on your evaluation.
5. **Implement**: Take action on the decision.
6. **Monitor**: Review the decision to ensure it is providing the desired outcome. Make adjustments if necessary.

Decision

Making a decision will affect our path in life. Consider all options before deciding so as to be informed. A decision might begin with an option like: *Do I take this job offer or the other offer? Which house do I buy or rent? Start a business or not start?* We make our decisions with our beliefs taken into consideration. Don't forget, our decisions are built on the foundation of our internal belief system.

A choice seems difficult to comprehend as we often blame others or our environment for what is in front of us. For example, if we have been asked to complete a project by a specific date, yet we still haven't finished it the day before, and we are up all night to complete it in time —who do we blame? Is it ourselves for procrastinating that we didn't want to complete the assignment, or do we complain that not enough time was given to us to finalise it? Either way we look at it, we can learn a lesson from the pressure we have felt.

How could we have made this simpler for us? If we broke down the project so we could complete certain aspects first, would we be better prepared sooner? Could we have asked for help from our coworkers, friends and other students who could have explained it better to us?

Looking at a grandfather clock, we see the pendulum swinging from side to side. Second to second. The minutes tick by loudly, and then an hour has passed, and the clock will chime. If it is a cuckoo clock, the bird will pop out to let us know another hour has passed. This is a visual representation of the repetitive nature of time; we can measure and count time in this way. Some may say hearing the clock ticking in the background can be therapeutic, and that may be so. Still, to others, the sound of time ticking away can make them fearful of what is coming next. Each tick is what you are experiencing now. It will eventually reach the next cycle of twenty-four hours—a new day, a new dawn and a new beginning.

Deepak Chopra said, *'I have all the time in the world. I am in touch with the timeless. I am surrounded by infinity. When I think like that, it doesn't mean I'm going to miss my train; it just means that I'm not thinking about it right now because I'm speaking to you'.*

Each rising day brings new experiences, new feelings and new emotions. Plans that we may have made months ago eventuate because time has moved forward to make our plans the present.

Time will always move forward; it cannot move back. The clock does not tick backwards. We all pass the minutes, hours and days, and we age and have experiences until we are no longer on this Earth. The time will still move forward and continue with or without us. It is there to help us create what we want as it is measurable and describable. We can reference time to assist us in expressing what we can see and do. This is why what we choose to do with our time on this Earth is so important, as we are the ones who are living life. It is our story that we are creating now.

QUANTUM THEORY

What if we now start looking at quantum mechanics? Quantum mechanics is a science dealing with the behaviour of matter and light on the atomic and subatomic scale. It attempts to describe and account for the properties of molecules and atoms and their constituents—electrons, protons, neutrons and other more esoteric particles such as quarks and gluons. According to *Encyclopaedia Britannica*, these properties include the interactions of particles with one another and with electromagnetic radiation (light, X-rays and gamma rays). Are we the subjects embedded in this universe? In the quantum realm, does it mean that matter can travel backwards and forwards? Time does not work the same as here on Earth. Can we then travel in time? In an article by Darren Orf titled 'Scientists Discovered How to Speed up Time. Seriously' (2023), the author presents research about a way to change the flow of time in a quantum system. They can speed it up, slow it down or reverse it. This isn't exactly time travel. It's using or reverting to different quantum states from different points in time. Scientists are questioning and exploring the warping of time to this day and trying to determine whether we can time travel.

Once we understand how time works, we can use it to our advantage by not letting it control our lives. We often say that we seek freedom from many situations and things, but if we are free from the restraints of time, then we are truly free.

REALITY

'There is no underlying reality to the world. 'Reality',
in the everyday sense, is not a good way to think
about the behaviour of the fundamental particles that
make up the universe; yet at the same time, those
particles seem to be inseparably connected into some
invisible whole, each aware of what happens to the
others'. — John Gribbin

What is this reality that we live in? It is hard to imagine that this reality
may not be what we initially believed. Are we in a matrix where we
subconsciously follow a blueprint? Or do we consciously see reality?
Albert Einstein said, *'Reality is merely an illusion, albeit a very persistent one'.* Is our reality an illusion because we cannot see beyond the
reality that we are in; are we stuck in our perception of reality?

The reality we experience is not an objective truth but a subjective
perception. As Deepak Chopra aptly put it, *'Perceptual reality is
different for different species. In some species, it is a way of observation. So, what we call scientific fact is not the ultimate truth. It is a
perceptual experience, and it's a way of observation'.* Our under-

standing of the world is not a reflection of absolute reality. It is a product of our perceptions. As Georgi Y. Johnson noted, *'Perception does not define who we are, but it does define where we are limited and where we are not yet free'*. If our perceptions can limit us, then is our view of reality also limited by our perception? Now, there's a brain tangle!

If this is the case, everyone's reality would then be different. Each of us has a variety of experiences in our lifetime. So, one person's perception would differ from others.

UNDERSTANDING REALITY AND FREQUENCY

We shape our reality by the frequency at which we operate. This physics-based idea suggests that the particles around us can change. They can align with our personal frequency. A high frequency, marked by love and gratitude, attracts a better reality. A low frequency, full of fear and worry, does not. High-frequency vibrations facilitate positive manifestations, while low-frequency vibrations can hinder them.

SUBJECTIVITY OF REALITY

Let's use a scenario to illustrate the subjectivity of reality. Imagine four people who were all present at the same time and place witnessed an event. Afterwards, they are asked to recount their memories of the event. This scenario has limited physical facts.

Each person believes their recounting is the accurate one. Three of them have similar accounts. The fourth person has a very different one. If we examine each person thoroughly, we may find a plausible truth, but it will still be an educated guess. What if the three with the shared memory convinced the fourth to agree with their version? This person might doubt themselves. They heard the same story from three people with no reason to lie. Would this person then question their own reality? Would they wonder if they were going mad?

MANIFESTATION FROM OTHER DIMENSIONS

The idea of manifesting desires from other dimensions challenges a fixed reality. If particles can change with our vibrations, we can reshape our reality. This raises profound questions about what is real and whether our current reality is the absolute endpoint.

PERCEPTION OF TIME

Our perception of reality is closely tied to our understanding of time. While future goals are yet to be realised, the present moment is our reality. Life shapes our reality. Our experiences, thoughts and emotions shape it. Recognising this can empower us to change our future by altering our current state of mind.

No matter what form we are in, the past, present and future all happen simultaneously. The present moment, or 'now', is how we perceive reality. We could improve our lives if we knew what was amiss in our past or present lives. Our feelings, thoughts, relationships and events shape our reality. That's why it is subjective. We can see and measure it when we compare it to objective reality, which is more solid. For instance, a rock is a rock, but this can also be subjective since the rock could be sand or a mountain. Everything is subjective to the person who sees it.

ROSE-COLOURED GLASSES

The term 'rose-coloured glasses' isn't about eyewear. This metaphor describes an optimistic worldview, not tinted lenses. It means seeing the world in a good way, even when things are tough. Many people think this is a silly or impossible way to see the world. But what if I told you it's not impossible? Why should we have a different view of the world? Think about how happy and bright our lives would be if we decided to see things this way. Can you change how you see the world so that you can see it this way?

CHANGING PERSPECTIVES

To put it another way, if we look at the world through a dark lens, we see it in a bad way. After that, we would have to determine why this is our world. What made us think that the world is bad? Did bad things happen to us in the past? What changed this view of reality to be so skewed? Sometimes, our actions and worldviews are influenced by past-life experiences rather than the present.

THE SYMBOLISM OF MOVEMENT

Imagine your left leg trailing behind your right leg as it moves forward. This symbolises leaving the past behind and advancing into the future. Our bodies can divide metaphorically between the right and left sides. The future is on the right, and the past is on the left. This imagery shows that our past and future are linked yet distinct. They are both parts of our existence.

LISTENING TO OUR HIGHER SELVES

What if I told you that our higher selves send us signals through our bodies? They do this to encourage us to notice and pay attention to the world around us. When combined with other conditions we may be experiencing, we get messages from our higher self. In Part Two, 'Emotions and Ailments', I explore the mind-body connection. We get signals, like gut feelings, to help us notice and solve situations.

Energetic Awareness

Checking our energy and surroundings can help us spot bad energy. By sensing our vibrations, we can maintain a high frequency, bringing us positive experiences and manifestations.

Multiple Dimensions

Have you ever heard the adage, '*All that is, is energy*'? Imagine that there are multiple dimensions. In them, many versions of us are living.

When we manifest, we claim from another dimension a reality, acting out what we desire. The future hasn't happened yet. But, when we self-actualise, we know we can change our future. We have the power and the agency to do it.

Our reality is a complex interplay of vibrations, perceptions and dimensions. Positive thoughts and emotions can raise our frequency. This can shape our experiences and help us manifest our desires. Other dimensions may influence it. We can then challenge and reshape our perception of existence. With awareness and mindfulness, we can control and enjoy life. Our world as we know it is shifting along with our timeframes.

We have all the answers within us, and it's time to dig deep. We may have grown up in an environment that tells us we can't access our desires and life paths. But we forget we were born with imagination, creativity and a divine spark. They activate our lives.

This will ensure the best possible future and the most efficient timetable for the here and now. Everything we do has so many opportunities, lessons and ways to improve, and we have beautiful choices to educate and become wise. Referring to Part Two, you can apply the techniques to enhance your perspective on the world. Everything is connected and relative.

PAST, PRESENT, FUTURE

 'Time is a continuous circle: the past, present and future are one and the same, waiting to be understood'. — Lao Tzu

Eckhart Tolle's book, *The Power of Now: A Guide to Spiritual Enlightenment*, emphasises the power of the present moment. We must learn to appreciate and live in the now, as it shapes our future.

We often dwell on our past, shaping our recollections. What if our present and past narratives were different? We might possess distinct memories or revised past stories. How accurately do we remember our past?

Can we recall a memory moment by moment? Can we share a memory and have the same recollection? Or do we struggle to remember what they are saying?

In *Signs You're Living in the Past*, Dr Suri and his colleagues argue that the past should be for reflection, not escape. Living in the past means being attached to childhood memories, self-blame, bitterness, fear of change and holding grudges.

What if I told you that you may have changed your past and no longer remember it, leading you to doubt its existence? To you, the person recalling the event might seem to be embellishing it. Recollections are often exaggerated. Is it right to remember a different version of the same incident as the truth? Could you both be right, having experienced variations of the same occurrence?

Could this suggest that our history has variations? Is one person's account of history different from another's? Which version is correct? Is this just one person's perspective on the situation? What if a third, fourth or fifth person has a different account of the event? Are they all correct? Who has an accurate recollection? This implies that any moment can have infinite outcomes, including days, years and events. As I mentioned in the last chapter, an alternative interpretation of reality can be at play.

Everyone can change the course of their lives. We all have the option to do as we please. The life you are now leading may not benefit you or those around you. The choices you make may tempt you down the rabbit hole. If you want to change, you must reconsider these tempting instant rewards. Why have you always followed this path? Is this your ego?

In the chapter 'Leave Your Ego at the Door', we explore how to choose the road with the least resistance and energy. Is it difficult to turn your back on this life and everything that comes with it?

According to Walsh et al., '*The reality we see reflects our consciousness. We can never explore reality without also exploring ourselves. This is because we are, and we create the reality we explore*'. Changes made in the present, such as instant choices, impact the future, not decisions made in the past. You have the power to change your future right now.

How can we change our story for the future and not repeat the lessons we don't need to keep learning? How do we break the loop?

Tune In to the Present

Imagine tuning into the now, the present moment, as if it were a radio station. Like a radio, you can only listen to one station at a time. The station you choose represents the reality you are experiencing.

Life allows presence in a single moment, no more. This is where you want to make decisions without letting your history influence you.

Resist the desire to repeat bad decisions. Say you've always wanted to steal vehicles. You are always tempted to take the next job. You can't get enough of the thrill and money that come with it. Then, you should take a deep breath, pause and consider what you can do to change. What can you use as a barrier to fight the temptation? If not resisting temptation means losing guardianship of your children, is it worthwhile? Can you overcome the problems you confront and recognise your own worth? You deserve a life of self-love and compassion.

Manifest the Life You Want

The first stage is to decide what you want out of life. Then, use one of the strategies from the 'Manifestation' chapter. For example, create a vision board, meditate or release negativity. The goal is to picture your ideal life. Then, make the needed changes now to achieve it. You must make these changes to allow the manifestation to enter your life. A life filled with negativity and bad decisions leaves no room for the optimistic new you.

Let Go of Any Beliefs or Feelings Holding You Back

When we live in the present, we must also let go of old beliefs and emotions. They stop us from claiming the life we want. If we believe we will never have enough money, this is our reality. We have a lot of feelings about money, and our devotion to it will only leave us with less money than we want. The more favourable our attitude and emotions about money, the more we will have. If we assume we will always have enough, this will be the fact. If we believe we will never have enough, that is our reality. When we let go of our thoughts and emotions about money or anything else, we allow great energy into our lives.

Appreciate What You Have

Every day, we can express gratitude for what we have. When we are grateful, more follows! Gratitude is infectious for those who feel good vibes and chemistry in our bodies. The 'Gratitude' chapter discusses many ways to exhibit thankfulness daily.

Live Without Being a Prisoner of Fear

Imagine if we could eliminate all our unwanted worries in life. The stress and concern would be eliminated. Fear of the future can keep us on the edge of our seats. It's like watching a suspenseful movie. We nibble popcorn and are addicted to what happens next. Our hearts are racing, our cortisol levels are high, and we are glued to the TV or cinema screens.

Can we imagine a life without disappointment? We fear bad grades, rejection from a crush or disapproval from a boss. So many what-ifs; can we live our lives terrified of what might happen? I say we can't.

We must examine what causes us dread. We must transmute this into a higher vibration. Not fearing what might happen means not fearing the future. It will let us live the life we want with joy.

Embrace the Present

Someone once asked me, '*You are all living in the present. How do you do this? It's a battle for me*'. He couldn't focus on the present moment since he constantly thought about the future and what lies ahead. My response was that I live in the now, and you are battling with it because you are living in the future. We must learn to live in the present moment. This is so the route can be opened. We can't open the path with the least resistance if we reject living in the present and focus on the future and the past.

If we focus on today and decide to live it fully, we will have a day full of rewards.

Letting Go

We have heard many times that we must let go. When we let go, the path we are aligned with will reveal itself.

We may struggle because there are so many obstacles on the road that we believe we must follow. Letting go is also about change. Many of us are stuck on the same hamster wheel. Go ahead and shake things up. Change our meals, exercise at different times of the day and go out during the week. Challenge ourselves to break our routines. Make room for excitement. This is the key to changing our vibration to lead us to experience life in the best possible way.

Taking Time for yourself

Set aside time to spend with family or rest your body and mind. Even if you can get away for a short time, such as a weekend, this can give you some relaxation. It doesn't need to be full of adventures.

Every day, we can connect with nature and use the tools we now have access to self-actualise.

CROSSING OVER

Trigger Warning: this next chapter contains topics around death and passing over.

 'Even though our rational mind has been trained to believe that when a person dies his spirit is gone, the truth is that the spirit does not die, it simply changes form. Your spirit can't die because it has no boundaries, no beginning and no end'. — **Wayne Dyer**

When the time has come, we will eventually cross over to the spirit realm. Our soul leaves our physical body and goes to heaven. In our society, it is commonly accepted that there are spirits and that our loved ones are there on the other side watching over us.

When our loved ones are crossing over, they experience immense love and welcome from friends and family who have already passed away. To ease the transition, they are there waiting for them. If they have been ill, their pain will go away as they transition back to their source. Seeing the loved ones they have missed in this lifetime is of great joy and comfort to the soul passing over.

It is a time to review their lifetime and all the lessons they have learned and have not learned. They look at the contract they signed as a soul before going into the human body to see if they had fulfilled it and whether they had accomplished everything there was to do. Did their journey change? Did they follow their free will and refuse part of the contract during their life journey? Did this refusal enhance what they had to learn or hold them back? There are so many questions that are asked and reviewed at this point. If they have not learned the lessons they were meant to in this lifetime on Earth, sometimes they will continue to expand and learn that lesson in the spirit realm.

Some souls have trouble crossing over as they don't want to leave their loved ones here on Earth, even though they can see the light on the other side. I was once at the funeral of a dear friend's father. Her mother had passed away some years prior, and we knew that she would be there waiting for him, as they loved each other very much. A huge wind picked up just before the end of the ceremony. The wind was so strong that the priest couldn't speak. The pages in his book were flapping. Did this mean that her father didn't want to leave the family? If this was so, he certainly was trying his hardest to get everyone's attention. Suddenly, the wind settled down, which signified that he moved on to the light. Even at the last moment, there is free will. It is up to the soul to decide whether they are leaving or staying here in spirit.

Another reason a spirit may have trouble moving on is that it may still feel that they have some unfinished business. This can be due to them passing quickly and unexpectedly or still not believing that they have passed. Others may not think they are worthy to move on due to their lifestyle here on Earth or their beliefs around worthiness. If they do not move on, they still have thoughts and emotions, the same as if they were still living. All souls are worthy of going to heaven, and they must realise this before they transition, no matter what. These souls need to let go and move across, but if they are here for a while, they can then become stuck and not know how to transition.

William Shakespeare said: *'All the world's a stage, and all the men and women merely players: they have their exits and their entrances; and one man in his time plays many parts, his acts being seven ages'.*

Over our lifespan, there are points that we can take to exit this life because we have free will. These exit points would have been added to our life contract when we created it with our higher self and guides. There are various reasons why these points were created, and one is that the lesson we need to learn is too challenging for us. If we decide to leave for that reason, we will be back as we have shortened the initial life contract we made when we came here on Earth. Another reason is our mission or purpose when we came to Earth may be completed early, and then our soul is given the choice of whether to stay or go. Some souls still choose to stay even if they have completed their mission, as they enjoy being here.

The exit points may be a serious health issue or an accident that seems like a near miss. If our soul decides to stay in these situations, we may feel that we are lucky to be alive. Sometimes, it can take a lifetime or many lifetimes to fully understand the concepts that we must learn. There are also some souls whose contract is for a short time, which differs from the exit point.

NEAR-DEATH EXPERIENCE

Near-death experiences (NDE) are the exact points that people have encountered. They have arrived at the exit. They may have tried to decide to leave. But, when they are in the NDE, they are jolted back into this reality. It is not their time yet. They have a mission here on Earth that is bigger than them. At this time, they may also decide they are not ready to cross over. But they are shown the other side and reminded that whatever is there will always be there waiting for them. In the article by Jefferey Long, 'Near-Death Experience. Evidence for Their Reality' (2014), he presents evidence for NDEs. An NDE happens when there is an experience during which the person is 'usually unconscious, comatose, or clinically dead'. Of the 278 NDErs,

54.7 per cent made significant life changes after the NDE. They then surveyed 1,122 NDErs, including scientists, physicians, attorneys and nurses and 962 (95.6 per cent) said the experience was real. He said: 'These findings suggest that most of us have not had an NDE. We should be very cautious about calling NDEs "unreal". Given that such a high percentage of NDErs consider their experiences to be "definitely real", it would be reasonable to accept their assessment of the reality of their personal experience unless there is good evidence that their experiences were not real'

The same study examines OBE's. 'About 45 per cent of NDE experiencers have an out-of-body experience (OBE). This is when the consciousness separates from the physical body. They can see and hear what is happening around them, but they are apart or above their physical body.' According to Long, some also have a life review. This study found that of the 617 NDEs, 14 per cent had a life review. 'NDErs typically describe their life review from a third-person perspective. The life review may include awareness of what others were feeling and thinking at the time earlier in their life when they interacted with them. This previously unknown awareness of what other people were feeling or thinking when they interacted with them is often surprising and unexpected to the NDErs'.

SOME THINGS THAT WE CAN DO TO EASE THE PAIN OF A LOVED ONE PASSING:

Having a loved one pass is truly one of the hardest things that we face in our lives. It doesn't matter who they are; it just means they matter so much to us. Our grief is a reflection of the love we have for them. It can take some people years not to feel the heartache every time they think of their loved one. Some things that we can think about to ease the pain for ourselves are as follows:

- If they were in pain, then they are not experiencing this anymore. They are free from it.

- They are with their loved ones who have already passed over.
- Their spirit guides welcome them.
- They are always with us, especially if we need their help.

The most considerable help we can give loved ones who are close to passing is to allow them to go. It is easy to beg them not to leave us, but when it is time, we can lovingly say goodbye to them. Before passing on, permitting them to go if they are ready can very much ease that transition. If they pass away unexpectedly, it is harder to come to terms with the incident and the passing. Maybe you keep thinking they would not have passed if certain things had not happened. As tough as this sounds, we must learn to let them go. Give them the freedom to move on. It will allow them to become whole again with their higher self and soul in the spirit realm.

This time can become a catalyst for questioning our mortality, who we are and the nature of our existence in this world. When we explore the meaning of life, it can be a time to reflect on how we can improve. For others, it can be a wake-up call. Mortality invites us to consider that we review even our relationships. We all want to live a life without regrets. When it is time for us to leave Earth, we want to be able to look back and say, '*I did everything I wanted to do, and I am happy to go*'.

BELOW ARE SOME WAYS THAT YOU CAN FEEL CONNECTED TO YOUR LOVED ONE WHO HAS PASSED ON:

Do a Run or Walk with a Charity

Many cities have charity fun runs or walks. You can join one to honour your loved one. If they passed with an illness, then pick a charity that raises money for their disease. In Melbourne, we have the Olivia Newton-John Cancer & Wellness Research Centre. They have hosted Walks for Wellness.

Reminisce with Friends and Family

Bring out the coffee and cake. Invite friends or family around to celebrate their life. This is especially true if it is their anniversary. It is a time to be together, reminisce and cherish the time that you had together. We've talked about Mum's cooking. We've discussed her favourite recipes and the stories she would tell when we got together.

Create a Photo Book

Photos can be anywhere, especially old ones. Gather the photos, whether they're physical or on hard drives, mobile phones or SD cards. Select your favourite ones and make an album to remind you of the great times you had together. This is especially therapeutic if you're missing them. You can also add quotes and sayings that they always said, as we all have a few. Otherwise, you can select a photo, put it in a frame and have it next to you.

Tick a Bucket List Item in Honour of Them

The bucket list can be yours. You can choose something that is in honour of them. Or it can be something you knew was on their list. This is a way that you can laugh and enjoy the moment, remembering what they would have loved or hated on the adventure.

Use the Belongings That Were Left to You

These items don't need to be anything big or valuable; they must be something they left you that reminds you of them. Looking at it or using it, whether it's clothing or a book, etc. There are many things you can have that can remind you of them.

MESSAGES AND SIGNS THAT OUR LOVED ONES ARE THERE

We can also talk to them even if they're not here, as they can hear us. Ask for signs that they're around.

Smelling something can remind you of loved ones. Do you smell coffee, roses or sometimes even cigarettes, but these items are nowhere to be seen? This is a loved one being near and trying to get your attention, telling you they're there with you. Some of us have this experience often, and others don't smell anything at all. This could mean you're okay and don't need reassurance that the loved one is okay. Or you're not tuning into the smells and messages around you.

In the 'Dreams' chapter, I also mention how the spirit can come to you in a dream.

Seeing things that remind us of our loved ones is also a sign they may be reaching out to us. My mother passed away in September 2021, and I was in my office by myself during the Christmas break, which was on the second floor. Every time I looked out of the window, I could see a butterfly. It would stay there for a while, then fly away and return. I felt like it was watching me, trying to get my attention. I felt that this was my mother coming to say hello; now, whenever I see butterflies, I think of her.

Feathers also remind me of her. We were on a family vacation in Hawaii, and we were on a tour. I exited the open truck and left my bag on the seat. When I returned, I picked up my bag and saw a feather underneath it. I'm unsure how it got there, but I just said hello to my mum. She was letting us know that she was there with us. So, butterflies and feathers are a lovely reminder of her.

A friend says she smells coffee for her mum and cigarettes for her dad. She finds comfort in that moment when she experiences this. It is amazing how, if we are in tune with what is happening around us, we can see and feel extraordinary things.

It is hard for us to imagine crossing over. Birth and death are guaranteed experiences when we have this human experience, and yet death brings so much fear. When we start to look beyond this world and lift our vibration, the pain may not leave; however, the understanding that our loved ones do indeed go on is a comfort.

AFTERWORD

I encourage everyone to embrace this journey of life with passion and determination. Anything truly rewarding will come with challenges, but when you reach your destination, you'll look back and know it was worth the ride. Along the way, you'll experience moments of pure bliss and joy, as well as times that test your resolve.

Understanding self-actualisation is the foundation of any spiritual or personal development journey. Life's ups and downs are essential; without them, we'd be bored. Is playing it safe indeed the way to live a life of purpose and meaning? Our souls crave wisdom and the thrill of discovery. This journey is an incredible adventure filled with lessons and growth.

Take small steps and be patient. Enjoy the process. Each of us has a unique path, so avoid comparisons and don't get caught up in someone else's journey. Find your tribe, those who allow you to be your authentic self. As you learn the lessons you came to this Earth to learn, you'll question if it was worth it. When you can answer 'Yes', you'll know you're living your best life.

Our consciousness must unite with others in love and compassion, for we are all interconnected. Our family, friends, acquaintances and even strangers are part of the one consciousness. The more we work on ourselves, the more we uplift the collective.

The pursuit of self-actualisation is a rewarding endeavour that enhances our quality of life and brings a sense of fulfilment and purpose. We are not seeking perfection; we seek alignment with our purpose, finding contentment and peace. A great spiritual reset is necessary, and the tools provided in this book can ease the journey.

Through this journey, we experience inner peace, clarity, calm, empathy and compassion for others. Above all, we experience love because we are all connected. In this state, we become the most authentic version of ourselves. We are one; everyone and everything is one.

Go for it—embrace the journey with all its highs and lows. It's worth it.

ACKNOWLEDGMENTS

I am deeply grateful to my family for accompanying me on this incredible journey.

To my children, your support and understanding have meant a great deal to me. Each of you has unique gifts that you have used to help me in this journey.

To my husband, Michael, your constant encouragement and support have been my guiding light. Your presence beside me throughout my journey of self-discovery has been a true blessing. Thank you for never wavering in your belief in me and standing steadfastly by my side. I extend my heartfelt appreciation to the remarkable individuals who have played a pivotal role in shaping my path. You know who you are, and your guidance and support have propelled me forward, and I am profoundly grateful for your presence in my life.

Special thanks to Kirsten, my publishing and creative consultant, whose expertise and dedication have transformed my vision into reality.

To all those who have contributed to this journey, whether through words of encouragement, moments of inspiration, or acts of kindness, I offer my deepest gratitude. This book is as much yours as it is mine.

RESOURCES:

Chapter One
Crandall, A., Powell, E. A., Bradford, G. C. *et al.* 'Maslow's Hierarchy of Needs as a Framework for Understanding Adolescent Depressive Symptoms Over Time.' *Journal of Child and Family Studies* 29, (2020): 273–81. https://doi.org/10.1007/s10826–019–01577–4.

Greene, L., and Burke, G. 'Beyond Self-Actualisation.' *Journal of Health and Human Services Administration* 30, no. 2 (2007): 116–128. https://doi.org/10.1177/107937390703000201.

Walsh, R. N., and Vaughan, F. 'Beyond the Ego: Toward Transpersonal Models of the Person and Psychotherapy.' *Journal of Humanistic Psychology* 20, no. 1 (1980): 5–31. https://doi.org/10.1177/002216788002000102

Chapter Two
Smith, J. 'Exploring Transpersonal Psychology: A Review.' *International Journal of Transpersonal Studies* 24, no. 1, (2007): 116–28. http://dx.doi.org/10.24972/ijts.2005.24.1.16.

Chapter Three
Gribbin, J. *In Search of the Multiverse: Parallel Worlds, Hidden Dimensions, and the Ultimate Quest for the Frontiers of Reality.* Hoboken: Wiley, 2010.
Gribbin, J. *In Search of Schrödinger's Cat: Quantum Physics and Reality.* New York: Bantam Books, 1984.
'Metaphysical.' In *Oxford Dictionary of Philosophy.* Oxford University Press, 2005. Retrieved from https://www.oxfordreference.com/display/10.1093/acref/9780198609810.001.0001/acref-9780198609810-e-4516.

Chapter Four
Bhetiwal, A. 'The Role of Musical Notes and Colour Frequencies for Balancing Chakras in the Human Body.' *International Journal for Research in Applied Science and Engineering Technology* 5, no. 8, (2017): 1556–61. https://doi.org/10.22214/ijraset.2017.8221.

Goldsby, T. L., Goldsby, M. E., McWalters, M., and Mills, P. J. 'Effects of Singing Bowl Sound Meditation on Mood, Tension, and Well-Being: An Observational Study.' *Journal of Evidence-Based Complementary & Alternative Medicine* 22, no. 3 (2017): 401–6. https://doi.org/10.1177/2156587216668109.

Hills, C. *Nuclear Evolution: Discovery of the Rainbow Body*. Boulder Creek: University of the Trees Press, 1977.

Landry, J. M. 'Physiological and Psychological Effects of a Himalayan Singing Bowl in Meditation Practice: A Quantitative Analysis.' *American Journal of Health Promotion* 28, no. 5, (2014): 306–9. https://doi.org/10.4278/ajhp.121031-ARB-528.

Marathe, C. D., and Acharya, J. 'Chakras, the Wheels of Life, a New Paradigm for Human Health, Relationship and Disease.' *International Journal of Mechanical and Production Engineering Research and Development* 10, no. 3 (2020): 4045–53. https://doi.org/10.24247/ijmperdjun2020383.

Selhub, E. 'Nutritional Psychiatry: Your Brain on Food.' *Harvard Health*, 18 September 2022. https://www.health.harvard.edu/blog/nutritional-psychiatry-your-brain-on-food-201511168626.

Chapter Five

Chellappa, S. L., Gordijn, M. C. M., and Cajochen, C. 'Can Light Make Us Bright? Effects of Light on Cognition and Sleep.' *Progress in Brain Research* 190 (2011): 119–33.

Holick, M. F. 'Sunlight and Vitamin D for Bone Health and Prevention of Autoimmune Diseases, Cancers, and Cardiovascular Disease.' *The American Journal of Clinical Nutrition* 80, no. 6 (2004): 1678S-88S. https://doi.org/10.1093/ajcn/80.6.1678S.

Pūtaiao, P. A. 'Waves and Energy: Energy Transfer.' *Science Learning Hub*. (2018). https://www.sciencelearn.org.nz/resources/2681-waves-and-energy-energy-transfer.

Chapter Six

Emmons, R. A., and McCullough, M. E. 'Counting Blessings Versus Burdens: An Experimental Investigation of Gratitude and Subjective Well-Being in Daily Life.' *Journal of Personality and Social Psychology* 84, no. 2 (2003): 377–89. https://psycnet.apa.org/doi/10.1037/0022–3514.84.2.377.

Jo, A., Iodice, S., et al. 'The Association Between Gratitude and Depression: A Meta-Analysis.' *International Journal of Depression and Anxiety* 4, no. 1 (2021). https://clinmedjournals.org/articles/ijda/international-journal-of-depression-and-anxiety-ijda-4-024.pdf

Jones, S. M., Bodie, G. D., and Hughes, S. D. 'The Impact of Mindfulness on Empathy, Active Listening, and Perceived Provisions of Emotional Support.' *Communication Research* 46, no. 6 (2019): 838–65. https://doi.org/10.1177/0093650215626983.

Pennebaker, J. W., and Chung, C. K. 'Expressive Writing: Connections to Physical and Mental Health.' In *The Oxford Handbook of Health Psychology*, edited by H. S. Friedman, 417–37. Oxford: Oxford University Press, 2011.

Toussaint, L., Nguyen, Q. A., Roettger, C., Dixon, K., Offenbächer, M., Kohls, N., Hirsch, J., and Sirois, F. 'Effectiveness of Progressive Muscle Relaxation, Deep Breathing, and Guided Imagery in Promoting Psychological and Physiological States of Relaxation.' *Evidence-Based Complementary and Alternative Medicine* (2021): 5924040. https://doi.org/10.1155/2021/5924040.

Wood, A. M., Joseph, S., Lloyd, J., and Atkins, S. 'Gratitude Influences Sleep Through the Mechanism of Pre-Sleep Cognitions.' *Journal of Psychosomatic Research* 66, no. 1 (2009): 43–8. https://doi.org/10.1016/j.jpsychores.2008.09.002.

Chapter Seven
Hölzel, B. K., Carmody, J., Vangel, M., Congleton, C., Yerramsetti, S. M., Gard, T., and Lazar, S. W. 'Mindfulness Practice Leads to Increases in Regional Brain Grey Matter Density.' *Psychiatry Research: Neuroimaging* 191, no. 1(2011): 36–43. https://doi.org/10.1016/j.pscychresns.2010.08.006.

Sharma, H. 'Meditation: Process and Effects.' *AYU (An International Quarterly Journal of Research in Ayurveda)* 36, no. 3 (2015): 233. https://doi.org/10.1016/j.pscychresns.2010.08.006.

Chapter Ten
National Institutes of Health Office of Dietary Supplements. 'Dietary Supplements: What You Need to Know.' *NIH Office of Dietary Supplements*, U.S. Department of Health and Human Services. Accessed 25 February 2024. https://ods.od.nih.gov/factsheets/WYNTK-Consumer/.

Mayo Clinic Staff. 'Anaphylaxis.' Mayo Clinic, 24 February 2024. https://www.mayoclinic.org/diseases-conditions/anaphylaxis/symptoms-causes/syc-20351468.

Michopoulou, Eleni and Jauniškis, Pijus. 'Exploring the Relationship Between Food and Spirituality: A Literature Review.' *International Journal of Hospitality Management* 87. (2020): 102494. https://doi.org/10.1016/j.ijhm.2020.102494.

World Health Organization. 'Micronutrients.' World Health Organization, 1 April 2024. https://www.who.int/health-topics/micronutrients"

Chapter Eleven

Borra, J. P., Roos, R. A., Renard, D., Lazar, H., Goldman, A., and Goldman, M. 'Electrical and Chemical Consequences of Point Discharges in a Forest During a Mist and a Thunderstorm.' *Journal of Physics D: Applied Physics* 30, no. 1 (1997): 84–93. https://doi.org/10.1088/0022–3727/30/1/011.

Jéquier, E., and Constant, F. 'Water as an Essential Nutrient: The Physiological Basis of Hydration.' *European Journal of Clinical Nutrition* 64, no. 2 (2009): 115–23. https://doi.org/10.1038/ejcn.2009.111.

Jiang, S. Y., Ma, A., and Ramachandran, S. 'Negative Air Ions and Their Effects on Human Health and Air Quality Improvement.' *International Journal of Molecular Sciences* 19, no. 10 (2018): 2966. https://doi.org/10.3390/ijms19102966.

Mohd Nani, S. Z., Majid, F. A., Jaafar, A. B., Mahdzir, A., & Musa, M. N. (2016). Potential Health Benefits of Deep Sea Water: A Review. *Evidence-based complementary and alternative medicine : eCAM, 2016,* 6520475. https://doi.org/10.1155/2016/6520475

Radin, D., Hayssen, G., Emoto, M., and Kizu, T. 'Double-Blind Test of the Effects of Distant Intention on Water Crystal Formation.' *Explore (NY)* 2, no. 5 (2006): 408–11. https://doi.org/10.1016/j.explore.2006.06.004.

White, M. P., Elliott, L. R., Gascon, M., Roberts, B., and Fleming, L. E. 'Blue Space, Health and Well-Being: A Narrative Overview and Synthesis of Potential Benefits.' *Environmental Research* 191, (2020): 110169. https://doi.org/10.1016/j.envres.2020.110169.

Chapter Twelve

Bratman, G. N., Daily, G. C., Levy, B. J., and Gross, J. J. 'The Benefits of Nature Experience: Improved Affect and Cognition.' *Landscape and Urban Planning* 138, (2015): 41–50. https://doi.org/10.1016/j.landurbplan.2015.02.005.

Grassini, S. 'The Benefits of Walking in Nature: A Review.' *Journal of Environmental Psychology* 30, no. 3 (2010): 201–230.

Li, Q. 'Effect of Forest Bathing Trips on Human Immune Function.' *Environmental Health and Preventive Medicine* 15, no. 1 (2010): 9–17. https://doi.org/10.1007/s12199–009–0083–8.

Li, Q., Otsuka, T., Kobayashi, M., Wakayama, Y., Inagaki, H., Katsumata, M. and Miyazaki, Y. 'Acute Effects of Walking in Forest Environments on Cardiovascular and Metabolic Parameters.' *European Journal of Applied Physiology* 99, no. 3 (2007): 212–18. https://doi.org/10.1007/s00421–006–0324–4.

Marselle, M. R., Hartig, T., Cox, D. T., de Bell, S., Knapp, S., Lindley, S., and Warber, S. L. 'Pathways Linking Biodiversity to Human Health: A Conceptual Framework.' *Environment International* 128 (2019): 101–19. https://doi.org/10.1016/j.envint.2019.04.016.

Park, B. J., Tsunetsugu, Y., Kasetani, T., Kagawa, T., and Miyazaki, Y. 'The Physiological Effects of Shinrin-yoku (Taking in the Forest Atmosphere or Forest Bathing): Evidence from Field Experiments in 24 Forests Across Japan.' *Environmental Health and Preventive Medicine* 15, no. 1 (2010): 18–26. https://doi.org/10.1007/s12199–009–0086–9.

Twohig-Bennett, C., and Jones, A. 'The Health Benefits of the Great Outdoors: A Systematic Review and Meta-Analysis of Greenspace Exposure and Health Outcomes.' *Environmental Research* 166 (2018): 628–37. https://doi.org/10.1016/j.envres.2018.06.030.

Ulrich, R. S., Simons, R. F., Losito, B. D., Fiorito, E., Miles, M. A., and Zelson, M. 'Stress Recovery During Exposure to Natural and Urban Environments.' *Journal of Environmental Psychology* 11, no. 3 (1991): 201–30. https://doi.org/10.1016/S0272–4944(05)80184–7.

Chapter Thirteen
Bratman, G. N., Daily, G. C., Levy, B. J., and Gross, J. J. 'The Benefits of Nature Experience: Improved Affect and Cognition.' *Landscape and Urban Planning* 138 (2015): 41–50. https://doi.org/10.1016/j.landurbplan.2015.02.005.

Grassini, S. 'The Benefits of Walking in Nature: A Review.' *Journal of Environmental Psychology* 30, no. 3 (2010): 201–30.

Kakunje, A., Sinha, A., and Archana, S. 'The Symbolic Meaning of Snakes in Dreams: A Psychoanalytic Approach.' *Indian Journal of Psychological Medicine* 41, no. 4 (2019): 382–6.

Li, Q. 'Effect of Forest Bathing Trips on Human Immune Function.' *Environmental Health and Preventive Medicine* 15, no. 1, (2010): 9–17. https://doi.org/10.1007/s12199–009–0083–8.

Li, Q., Otsuka, T., Kobayashi, M., Wakayama, Y., Inagaki, H., Katsumata, M. and Miyazaki, Y. 'Acute Effects of Walking in Forest Environments on Cardiovascular and Metabolic Parameters.' *European Journal of Applied Physiology* 99, no. 3 (2007): 212–18. https://doi.org/10.1007/s00421–006–0324–4.

Marselle, M. R., Hartig, T., Cox, D. T., de Bell, S., Knapp, S., Lindley, S., and Warber, S. L. 'Pathways Linking Biodiversity to Human Health: A Conceptual Framework.' *Environment International* 128 (2019): 101–19. https://doi.org/10.1016/j.envint.2019.04.016.

Nielsen, T., and Carr, M. 'Food and Dreams: Multicultural Perceptions.' *Frontiers in Psychology* 6 (2015): 1–15. https://doi.org/10.3389/fpsyg.2015.00472.

Park, B. J., Tsunetsugu, Y., Kasetani, T., Kagawa, T., and Miyazaki, Y. 'The Physiological Effects of Shinrin-yoku (Taking in the Forest Atmosphere or Forest Bathing): Evidence from Field Experiments in 24 Forests Across Japan.' *Environmental Health and Preventive Medicine* 15, no. 1 (2010): 18–26. https://doi.org/10.1007/s12199–009–0086–9.

Saunders, D. T., Roe, C. A., Smith, G., and Clegg, H. 'Lucid Dreaming Incidence: A Quality Effects Meta-Analysis of 50 Years of Research.' *Consciousness and Cognition* 43 (2016): 197–215. https://doi.org/10.1016/j.concog.2016.06.002.

Twohig-Bennett, C., and Jones, A. 'The Health Benefits of the Great Outdoors: A Systematic Review and Meta-Analysis of Greenspace Exposure and Health Outcomes.' *Environmental Research* 166 (2018): 628–37. https://doi.org/10.1016/j.envres.2018.06.030.

Chapter Fourteen
Joshi, A., Roy, S., Manik, R. K., and Sahoo, S. K. 'Scientific philosophy: Exploring Existential, Metaphysical, and Ethical Research Philosophy Behind the Question "Who am I?".' *Journal of Pharmaceutical Negative Results* 14, no. 3 (2023): 1648–71.

Chapter Fifteen
Walsh, R. N., and Vaughan, F. 'Beyond the Ego: Toward Transpersonal Models of the Person and Psychotherapy.' *Journal of Humanistic Psychology* 20, no. 1 (1980): 5–31. https://doi.org/10.1177/002216788002000102

Chapter Sixteen
Johns Hopkins Medicine. 'The Power of Positive Thinking.' Retrieved 18 May 2024, from https://www.hopkinsmedicine.org.

Lee, Y. S., Ryu, Y., Jung, W. M., Kim, J., Lee, T., and Chae, Y. 'Understanding Mind-Body Interaction from the Perspective of East Asian Medicine.' *Evidence-Based Complementary and Alternative Medicine: eCAM* (2017): https://doi.org/10.1155/2017/7618419.

Visco, V., Pietrosanti, M., Aniballi, E., Salemi, S., Santoni, A., and D'Amelio, R. 'Lymphocyte Subsets are Influenced by Positivity Levels in Healthy Subjects Before and After Mild Acute Stress.' *Immunology Letters* 188 (2017): 13–20. https://doi.org/10.1016/j.imlet.2017.05.012.

Chapter Seventeen
Daniel Amen
Website:_ https://www.amenclinics.com/

Amen, D. G. *Change Your Brain, Change Your Life (Revised and Expanded Edition): The Breakthrough Program for Conquering Anxiety, Depression, Obsessiveness, Lack of Focus, Anger, and Memory Problems.* Harmony, 2015.

Amen, D. G. *Change Your Brain, Change Your Life: The Breakthrough Program for Conquering Anxiety, Depression, Obsessiveness, Anger, and Impulsiveness.* Three Rivers Press, 1998.

Amen, D. G. *The End of Mental Illness: How Neuroscience is Transforming Psychiatry and Helping Prevent or Reverse Mood and Anxiety Disorders, ADHD, Addictions, PTSD, Psychosis, Personality Disorders, and More.* Tyndale Momentum, 2020.

Amen, D. G. *Magnificent Mind at any Age: Natural Ways to Unleash Your Brain's Maximum Potential.* Harmony, 2010.

Amen, D. G. *Memory Rescue: Supercharge Your Brain, Reverse Memory Loss, and Remember What Matters Most.* Tyndale Momentum, 2017.

Amen, D. G. *Unleash the Power of the Female Brain: Supercharging Yours for Better Health, Energy, Mood, Focus, and Sex.* Harmony, 2013.

Amen, D. G. *Use Your Brain to Change Your Age: Secrets to Look, Feel, and Think Younger Every Eay.* Crown Archetype, 2012.

Australian Bureau of Statistics. *National Health Survey.* 2022. Retrieved from https://www.abs.gov.au/statistics/health/health-conditions-and-risks/national-health-survey.

Australian Institute of Health and Welfare. *National Study of Mental Health and Wellbeing.* 2023. Retrieved from https://www.aihw.gov.au/reports/mental-health-services/national-study-of-mental-health-and-well-being.

Australian Institute of Health and Welfare. *Prevalence and Impact of Mental Illness.* 2023. Retrieved from https://www.aihw.gov.au/mental-health/overview/prevalence-and-impact-of-mental-illness

Chu, B., Marwaha, K., Sanvictores, T., Awosika, A. O., and Ayers, D. 'Physiology, Stress Reaction.' In *StatPearls*. StatPearls Publishing, 2024.

Judith Lewis Herman
Herman, J. L. *Father-Daughter Incest.* Harvard University Press, 1997.

Herman, J. L. *Incest Between Fathers and Daughters.* Harvard University Press, 1981.

Herman, J. L. *Trauma and Recovery: The Aftermath of Violence—from Domestic Abuse to Political Terror.* Basic Books, 1992.

Herman, J. L. *Trauma and Recovery: The Aftermath of Violence—from Domestic Abuse to Political Terror* (Revised ed.). Basic Books, 2015.

Herman, J. L. *Truth and Repair: How Trauma Survivors Envision Justice.* Basic Books, 2023.

Herman, J. L., & Schatzow, E. 'Recovery and Verification of Memories of Childhood Sexual Trauma.' In *Trauma and Recovery: The Aftermath of Violence—from Domestic Abuse to Political Terror.* Harvard University Press, 1987.

Melbourne Institute. *Household, Income and Labour Dynamics in Australia (HILDA) Survey.* 2021. Retrieved from https://melbourneinstitute.unimelb.edu.au/hilda.

Peter Levine
Website: https://www.somaticexperiencing.com

Levine, P. A. (1997). *Waking the tiger: Healing trauma.* North Atlantic Books.

Levine, P. A. (2010). *In an unspoken voice: How the body releases trauma and restores goodness.* North Atlantic Books.

Levine, P. A. (2015). *Trauma and memory: Brain and body in a search for the living past.* North Atlantic Books.

Levine, P. A., & Kline, M. (2007). *Trauma through a child's eyes: Awakening the ordinary miracle of healing.* North Atlantic Books.

Gabor Maté

Website: https://drgabormate.com

Maté, G. (2003). *When the body says no: The hidden cost of stress*. Vintage Canada.

Maté, G. (2010). *In the realm of hungry ghosts: Close encounters with addiction*. Vintage Canada.

Maté, G., & Maté, D. (2019). *Hold on to your kids: Why parents need to matter more than peers* (Updated ed.). Vintage Canada.

Maté, G. (2022). *The myth of normal: Trauma, illness, and healing in a toxic culture*. Avery.

Richard C. Schwartz

Website: **https://ifs-institute.com**

Schwartz, R. C. *Internal Family Systems Therapy*. Guilford Press, 1995.

Schwartz, R. C. *Introduction to the Internal Family Systems Model*. Trailheads Publications, 2001.

Schwartz, R. C., & Falconer, L. *The Enlarged Inner Self: Mindfulness and Self-Compassion in Internal Family Systems Therapy*. Guilford Press, 2002.

Schwartz, R. C., & Goulding, R. A. *The Mosaic Mind: Empowering the Tormented Selves of Child Abuse Survivors*. Norton, 1995.

Schwartz, R. C., & Sweezy, M. *Internal Family Systems Therapy: New Dimensions*. Routledge, 2013.

Schwartz, R. C., & Sweezy, M. *Internal Family Systems Therapy (2nd ed.)*. Guilford Press, 2019.

Schwartz, R. C. *No Bad Parts: Healing Trauma and Restoring Wholeness with the Internal Family Systems Model*. Sounds True, 2021.

Bessel van der Kolk

Website: https://www.besselvanderkolk.com/

Van der Kolk, B. A. *The Body Keeps the Score: Brain, Mind, and Body in the Healing of Trauma*. Viking, 2014.

Van der Kolk, B. A. 'The Compulsion to Repeat the Trauma: Re-enactment, Revictimization, and Masochism.' *Psychiatric Clinics of North America* 12, no. 2 (1994): 389–411.

Van der Kolk, B. A. (Ed.). *Post-Traumatic Stress Disorder: Psychological and Sequelae.* American Psychiatric Publishing, 1987.

Van der Kolk, B. A. *Psychological Trauma.* American Psychiatric Publishing, 1987.

Van der Kolk, B. A., and Greenberg, M. S. (Eds.). *The Psychobiology of Post-Traumatic Stress Disorder.* American Psychiatric Publishing, 1987.

Van der Kolk, B. A., McFarlane, A. C., and Weisaeth, L. (Eds.). *Traumatic Stress: The Effects of Overwhelming Experience on Mind, Body, and Society.* Guilford Press, 1996.

Chapter Eighteen

Orf, Darren. 'Scientists Discovered How to Speed Up Time. Seriously. We Can Reverse It, Too'. *Popular Mechanics.* 23 February 2023. www.popularmechanics.com/science/a43027951 'quantum-time-travel/.

Squires, Gordon Leslie. 'Quantum Mechanics'. *Encyclopædia Britannica.* Encyclopædia Britannica, Inc. 25 December 2023, www.britannica.com/science/quantum-mechanics-physics.

Chapter Twenty

Suri, R. K., & Yadav, U. 'Signs You're Living in the Past.' *Psycho Wellness Centre.* 2024. Retrieved from https://www.psychowellnesscenter.com/Blog/signs-you-re-living-in-the-past.

Walsh, R. N., and Vaughan, F. 'Beyond the Ego: Toward Transpersonal Models of the Person and Psychotherapy.' *Journal of Humanistic Psychology* 20, no. 1 (1980): 5–31. https://doi.org/10.1177/002216788002000102.

Chapter Twenty-One

Long, Jeffrey. 'Near-Death Experience. Evidence for Their Reality'. *Missouri Medicine*, US National Library of Medicine, 2014. http://www.ncbi.nlm.nih.gov/pmc/articles/PMC6172100/

ABOUT THE AUTHOR

Fiona Failla is an award-winning businesswoman whose spiritual quest for answers led her on an extraordinary path of deep learning and self-discovery. Realising the need for a beginner's guide, Fiona penned her first book, *Reality and Beyond This World: A Beginners Guide to Self-Actualisation*, demystifying complex concepts for those newly awakened to their spiritual journeys. Grounded in both personal experience and scientific research, the book provides easy-to-understand insights into everything from meditation, chakras, ego, dimensions, energy clearing and so much more.

Fiona's love for life is richly infused with new adventures and opportunities to grow and always learn. She finds joy in sharing connections with loved ones over a home-cooked meal, travelling the world, collecting crystals and enjoying nature. Through her book and her life's work, Fiona continues to be of service to others, helping others understand that transformation and connection are within reach for everyone.

facebook.com/Fiona-Failla-Writes

instagram.com/fionafaillawrites

tiktok.com/@fionafaillawrites

youtube.com/@FionaFailla

Printed in Australia
Ingram Content Group Australia Pty Ltd
AUHW011300151024
401275AU00005B/8